The Beast with Seven Heads and You

The Revelation 13 Beast Identified From the Historical Evidence

By

Wayne L. Atchison

Two Tassels Ministry

Published By: Two Tassels Ministry
1609 Lund Lane
Polson, Montana 59860

Two Tassels Ministry
www.YhwhIs1.com

First Edition
April 22, 2015
ISBN-13: 978-0-9962963-0-4
ISBN: 0996296301

Visit Two Tassels Ministry for updates.

Contents

FOREWORD

Worshipping the Beast Starts with Believing "The Lie"!

(Genesis 3:4; 2-Thessalonians 2:11)

The Beasts of Revelation 13 and its mark of "666" is a subject on the minds of many people. **This fully documented book is both a religious and a historical research presentation, based on the accumulated information from many historical sources**.

The primary purpose is to demonstrate the identity of the Revelation 13 "Beast with Seven Heads", its **Name**, its **Mark**, and its **seven Religious Systems**, by using archeological and historical references. The historical documentation demonstrates a worldwide cultural and religious deception far more pervasive than most understand.

The names, titles, and symbols we see around us are meant to tell us something. We see symbols on church buildings, and we sing songs using special names and titles. If you do not know what a name, title, or a symbol really means, **then you cannot be forewarned**. By having an understanding of the names, titles, and symbols used to represent the worship of the Great Dragon and his agents, you can be forewarned that something around you is just not right.

The Beast with Seven Heads and You

From the accumulated historical evidence **the riddle of the "666" is solved**, including the "**Name of the Beast**" and its **Mark**. This solution is **both fully documented, and historically validated** from numerous Mysteries, such as Babylonian, Egyptian, Greek, Roman, Hindu, Buddhist, Oriental, and Freemasonry. Ultimately, **you must understand what "The Lie" is**.

Many readers may feel overwhelmed upon realizing just how culturally pervasive and how commonly accepted is the worship of the Great Dragon, through his agents of the Beast with Seven Heads. The problem is, since the worship of the Great Dragon is so much a part of our culture and mindset, how do the worshippers of the God of Israel get out of this system, as instructed in Revelation 18:1-5?

This Book is fully referenced with 96 historical color images, and provides enough understanding of the names, titles, symbols, and **Marks** used by the Great Dragon, **to be forewarned**.

Most Often Cited References

These are itemized as they are the most often referenced sources.

"**REF A**": "**Stellar Theology and Masonic Astronomy**", by Robert Hewitt Brown, first published in 1882, ISBN 1-56459-357-6, available in Bookstores.

"**REF B**": "**The Two Babylons**", by Alexander Hislop, First published as a pamphlet in 1853 -- greatly expanded in 1858, available in Bookstores, search on highlighted text.
Text-only version: **https://archive.org/stream/theTwoBabylons/TheTwoBabylons_djvu.txt**
Text and Pictures version:
TheTwoBabylons#page/n0/mode/2up

"**REF C**": (**S:** "**full text of Visions of Hermes**"): **http://www.world-enlightenment.com/Mythology/Thoth-Hermes-Trismegistus/Visions-of-Hermes.html**), search on highlighted text.

"**REF D**": **"www.YhwhIs1.com/" plus the given additional link-text.**

Please Note:

- All images herein are not copyrighted, or are under "public domain", and were copied directly from the Internet under "fair use". Quotations have their authorship reference given.
- Using **the Wikipedia website** is very useful for getting some information fast, (**http://en.wikipedia.org**).
- "**(S:**" - means to do an Internet Search for the specified text.
- **When references are not provided**, it is because the information can be easily verified by simple Internet searches of the highlighted words being shown.
- The term "**planet**" will also refer to the Moon and the Sun as well. A planet will be these seven: the Sun, the Moon, Mercury, Venus, Mars, Jupiter, and Saturn.
- The term, "**The Mysteries**", is used to identify the cultural and religious Priesthoods of the Great Dragon, his agents, and his Revelation 13 Beast with Seven Heads. However, **the cultural and religious system of the Great Dragon is far more extensive and pervasive than just "The Mysteries"**.

Executive Summary

By bringing numerous historical references together, it is discovered that, from the highest level point of view, there are only two supernatural entities which claim to be the ultimate authority. Both supernatural entities are known by the very same titles, such as "**The Creator God**", "**The Supreme Being**", "**The Master Architect**", the "**Great Architect**", the "**Architect of All**", "**God The Father**", "**The Supreme Mind**", and "**The Divine Light**". These two supernatural entities have many personal names derived from the various languages and cultures, but for the purpose of this presentation they will be called the "**YHWH**" of the Hebrew/Aramaic Text, and the "**Great Dragon**" from the "**Visions of Hermes**" Text.

Some are familiar with the **YHWH** (is יהוה Hebrew-to-English, "YHVH" is Hebrew-to-German, YHWH is pronounced "Yahowah" in Aramaic) as written in the Hebrew/Aramaic Text. This Hebrew word is the name of the "God of Israel", as specified by Himself. For example: talking to Moses **the YHWH says** that יהוה (YHWH) **is His name forever**, and that His title is: "the Elohim/God of Abraham, the Elohim/God of Isaac, and the Elohim/God of Jacob, (Exodus 3:15).

It is this Hebrew name, YHWH, which is used over 6800 times in the Hebrew/Aramaic Text to identify the supernatural entity that is to be worshipped by all men. This supernatural Being is the only Elohim/God which will bring people back to life again, judge them for the good and bad deeds they did, and grant eternal life to those chosen as good, (Job 19:25-27; Isaiah 26:19; Ezekiel 37:3-14; Daniel 12).

In Biblical circles it is often asserted that "God is One". **But the Hebrew Text does not say that "God is One".**

The Hebrew Text says **that " YHWH is '1' "**!

> "Hear O'Isreal, YHWH our Elohim, **YHWH IS '1'**. And you shall love YHWH, your Elohim, with all of your heart, and with all of your soul, and with all of your might", (Deuteronomy 6:4-5, http://biblehub.com/interlinear/deuteronomy/6-4.htm,
> "**YHWH**" is Strong's H3068, and "**Elohim**" is H430. Two different words; "YHWH" is His name, and "Elohim" is a title that even men can be given).

When the Messiah Yahoshua (Aramaic, Greek 'Ieesous', English 'Jesus') recited this verse in Mark 12:29, He used the Greek word for the cardinal digit '**1**'. Thus, **the Messiah recited this verse as: " YHWH IS '1' "**.

Many are familiar with the "**Great Dragon**" referenced in the book of Revelation, but probably not by the name of "**Poimandres**" as given in the "**Visions of Hermes**" Text. As Poimandres describes himself in the "**Visions of Hermes**", this supernatural entity is manifested as the Great Dragon. For this reason we often see either the **Dragon** or the **Serpent** depicted in religious art and symbols found around the world.

From historical records a replicated statue of the goddess Artemis in her Temple at Ephesus. Notice "**The Serpent**" in lower-right.

Each of these two supernatural Beings has their own human priests, that is, their own Priesthood. Both Priesthoods have been around since Adam, throughout history, even to this day, **and have many branches** spread all over the world.

The YHWH has His own Priesthood through the line of Noah and Shem. This Priesthood of the YHWH has continued throughout history, and is called the "**Melchizedek Priesthood**" in both the Hebrew and the Greek Texts, (**http://en.wikipedia.org/wiki/Priesthood_of_Melchizedek**).

For example, the resurrected Messiah is called a "priest forever after the order of Melchizedek", (Hebrews 8:1). The Levitical Priesthood, authorized by the YHWH through Moses, is essentially a branch of the YHWH's "**Melchizedek Priesthood**", specifically authorized for their unique service to Israel.

The Great Dragon also has his own Priesthood through the line of (Adam . . . Noah, Ham) <u>Cush, Nimrod, and Horus</u>. Thus the Priesthood of the Great Dragon has existed throughout history. In this Priesthood Cush, Gaia, Isis, Nimrod, and Horus have been deified into the "primary gods", and are worshipped directly or indirectly using various names and myths found around the world. The primary human **agent of the Great Dragon is Cush** and the religious "**Schools of Thought**" that Cush started.

Many researchers use the term "**The Mysteries**" in an attempt to place a "label" onto this line of religious thought, (**www.factbook.org/wikipedia/en/m/my/mystery_religion.html**), however this label is actually too limiting in scope. The religious system of the Great Dragon is far more culturally and religiously pervasive than just "**The Mysteries**" as defined in dictionaries. Even so, this presentation will use this term, "**The Mysteries**", but primarily only to contrast between the Priesthoods of the YHWH and the Great Dragon.

With little effort it is verified that the YHWH expects people to worship only Himself. In the Hebrew Text it is very clear that the YHWH becomes quite upset when people do not seek Him for their spiritual enlightenment, help, and instruction. The contrast is that people look to the other choice, the Priesthood and deified gods of the Great Dragon, for their spiritual enlightenment, help, and instruction instead. The YHWH is very patient, but the focal issue is which supernatural entity is being sought for spiritual enlightenment, help, and instruction.

With two Priesthoods, the question is: "What exactly are the most significant differences between the two religious systems?" That is, what are the 'big deal' differences between the worship of the YHWH and the worship of the Great Dragon?

At the highest level **there are two primary differences**:

1.) "**Do you have an immortal soul?**": When your body dies, does your thinking and awareness keep on "living"?

2.) "**Which "Specific Laws" do you live by?**": Laws such as worship Me on the Sabbath or on the Sunday, are "**Specific Laws**". These laws say: "Do 'this' exact thing to honor Me". Laws such as "do not steal, do not murder" are not specific, as they present only conceptually "good things to do". The "**Specific Laws**" are verifiable separators. Part of the religious confusion is that **both supernatural Beings teach people to be "a good person"**. But each supernatural Being also has a "short list" of "**Specific Laws**" which unambiguously demonstrate which of the two supernatural Beings you are following.

The Beast with Seven Heads and You

The YHWH tells us in the Hebrew and Greek Texts that He alone is the only Being that has "**Immortality**" (1-Timothy 6:16), that is, we humans do not have an immortal soul that keeps on living after we die. We have to get that from the YHWH.

The Text teaches that when we die, all of our thinking and awareness stops, we are essentially asleep.

> "Behold, I shew you a mystery; We shall not all sleep, but we shall all be changed, In a moment, in the twinkling of an eye, at the last trump: for the trumpet shall sound, and the dead shall be raised incorruptible, and we shall be changed", (1-Corinthians 15:51-54).

In order to regain our thinking and awareness we must be resurrected, brought back to life again with a new body, and this is done only by the YHWH.

In contrast, the foundational teaching of the Great Dragon is that we humans do have an immortal soul that keeps on living after we die. This is the opposite teaching from that of the YHWH. This is exactly what the Serpent told Eve in the Garden: "the serpent said unto the woman, **Ye shall not surely die**", (Genesis 3:4).

Essentially,

> "**The Lie**" of the Great Dragon is his promising you that you are a composite of two parts, "a Physical Body and a Spiritual Mind", two separate things, wherein your "**Mind**" is immortal, and that your "**Body**" is earthly, and can never be immortal. Your afterlife will be **immortality in a new spiritual Body, without needing the YHWH to bring it about**.

In this the YHWH is not needed to give spiritual enlightenment, help, and instruction, and the YHWH is not needed to bring anyone back to life again. Guided by the concept that souls keep living after death, people can experience both "the good and the evil" aspects of making their own decisions on daily conduct, without the fear of the YHWH, or the fear of dying forever.

Using the central foundation of the "**immortality of the soul**" the populous can be exploited by the priests. The Priesthood, guided by this concept of immortality, can tell people to give them money, or to "do things" so that a dead relative can get out of some state of Purgatory, or to get past a certain gate. People can call upon the dead to "do things", such as enforce spells and curses. They can scare people that some things are haunted by the "**Spirits of the Dead**". The priests can tell people to pray to those who had died for help and instructions, because they are still alive and will "do things" for them. Examples of this are prayers given to Mary, dead relatives, and to the Saints.

The ultimate ramification of the central issue of the "**immortality of the soul**" is very startling. Stated simply: if it be a cosmic fact that the YHWH is the only supernatural Being that can bring the dead back to life and awareness again, and that the Great Dragon cannot do this, then **the ultimate ramification of believing the "Great Dragon", is that of oblivion**. That is, if the YHWH is right, then those that rely upon the Great Dragon's promise for the immortality of their souls will simply be no more.

Thus, we perceive the grand goal of the Great Dragon, the Adversary to the YHWH. Ultimately, **his goal is the unfulfilled potential, and the literal oblivion** of those created in the image of the YHWH. Fortunately, the YHWH, through His resurrected and exalted Son Yahoshua the Messiah, **has a grand plan to save our eternity**.

By understanding the names, titles, symbols, and Marks used by the Great Dragon and his agents, you will be able to see the signals of his worship system, **and thereby be forewarned**.

The YHWH, and His resurrected Son Yahoshua, want everyone to wake up and see what is going on. Seek the YHWH **with your whole heart**, and obey His "**Specific Laws**", **because you want to**.

First Things First, What Are You?

First let us get something out of the way right up front. There is only one thing that you know for sure. That is: "**You Know That You Exist**!" All other information comes from external sources. You can prove it, this way.

When you are ready, just close your eyes, just for about twenty seconds. Try to limit all inputs from your five senses. Cover your nose, plug your ears, keep your mouth shut without food, and ignore whatever is touching you. What you are left with is "The You". Even without the body's senses, no inputs from the five senses, "The You" is still thinking. You do not need your body's sensory inputs to think about fixing dinner, what you will say to apologize for something you did, how angry you were when they said 'that', and how happy you are with your new tools. That is, "The You" includes all of your memories, your expectations, your personality, your likes, and your dislikes. Your thinking and awareness are there, and you know that they are there. You know that "The You" exists even when your bodily inputs are being ignored. The only body part "The You" needs is your brain.

The fundamental question centered on the issue of "Do you have an immortal soul?" is this: when your body dies and all of its functionality stops, does your thinking and awareness stop too, or, are you somehow able to keep on thinking with awareness, even outside of your dead body, even without your physical brain?

More than Just Existing

There is more to "What Are You" than just "Existing". When you reopen your eyes, and allow the body's five senses to input data again, then you will also realize something else very important. You will experience that "The You" includes both your body and your mind. Your thinking and awareness are directly tied to the inputs received from your body.

Everything that you know or can think about, your thinking, and your awareness, are all affected by your five senses, and are all processed inside of your physical brain. If something damages your physical brain, then you will simply stop thinking correctly. If your physical brain is damaged then "The You" is compromised. Impacts might be that your five senses may be impaired, some of your ability to think may be impaired, some of your awareness may disappear, and you may stop knowing as much as you did before it was damaged. Thus, "The You" is directly dependent upon your physical brain and inputs. That is, **"The You" needs a body**!

In the Egyptian Mysteries, the immortal soul lives on into the afterlife, but still needs a new body to be whole again. Even a non-corporeal body is better than no body at all.

The Egyptian Mysteries separates a person into five parts:

The "**Ren**": A unique name given at birth.

The "**Sheut**": The person's shadow.

The "**Ib**": The seat of emotion, thought, will, intention, good or bad.

The "**Ba**": Everything that makes a person unique, the personality, the soul.

The "**Ka**": The vital essence, the difference between a living and a dead person. The vital essence is a "**light-body**", and is fed by the physical offerings made to that person.

Two more parts complete the concept of life after death:

The "**Khat**": Your physical body, but it is now dead and decaying.

The "**Akh**": The person's non-corporeal entity, having intellect, living on in the afterlife. The Egyptian Mysteries teach that after death the Ba and Ka must somehow be reunited, in order to reanimate the person's Akh, which essentially is his living thinking immortal soul. In the afterlife the Ka and Ba still needs a body to be fully alive, to be an Akh.

(**http://en.wikipedia.org/wiki/Ancient_Egyptian_concept_of_the_soul**).

The Catholic catechism teaches that the resurrection is the **reunion** of "the immortal soul" with the "glorified body". This reunion reunites a person's identity, entirety, and immortality, (**www.catholic.com/encyclopedia/heaven**).

Nearly all religions, whether derived from worshipping the YHWH or the Great Dragon, have the same ultimate goal. Somehow, **there is a path by which "The You" is given another new body** of some kind, so that "The You" will be fully whole once again. After all, you can engage in "just thinking" for a very long time, **but you must have some kind of a body in order to do anything about it**.

The Christians call this path "a resurrection". Some religions have a path called "reincarnation". Many religions have "an afterlife journey", in which "The You" without a body must somehow traverse differing celestial obstacles before getting some kind of a new body again.

Therefore, the answer to "What Are You?" is that **you are "a thinking and aware entity" with "a physical body" to do things with**. At death the thinking and aware entity is either halted or separated from the dead fleshly body. For the purposes of this presentation, the thinking and aware entity will be called the "**The You**", and your body will be called simply the "**Body**".

Asking the religious question again, "Do we have an immortal soul?", can now be rephrased: "After death, does "The You" keep on, or, does the "The You" stop?" Either way you answer this question, it remains that after death the goal is to have some way so that "The You" is given another new body, so that "The You" can be whole again, and do things.

Another Point about "What You Are"

There is another point to make about "What You Are". Close your eyes again, just as before. This time start to pray. Being religious or not makes no difference to making this point. After you started to pray, then stop at any time. The point is that by making that prayer attempt, what happened is **"The You" wanted to mentally contact someone else that is external to you**. "**The You**" reached outside of itself to talk to someone else having enough intellect to hear and understand. Further, you wanted that external entity to not only hear and understand what you were saying, but also have the power to grant any requests you made.

Most would call this external entity you are trying to talk to "your god". That is, the external entity "The You" looks to for spiritual enlightenment, help, and instruction. If you are trying to talk to "your god", it is manifest that who ever you are talking to; **you also want that deity to somehow help in the task of putting you back together again after death**. Of course the question is: "To which external entity do you talk to for help, instruction, and for putting "The You" back into a new body again?"

Did you talk to the YHWH, or to the Great Dragon?

But words are "cheap". If you are doing the things the Great Dragon wants you to do to show you are worshipping him, but think in your heart that you are praying to the YHWH, what does your confused worship mixture mean to those people watching, and to the YHWH?

One of the overwhelming ramifications of this presentation is that **it does not matter what you think in your heart!** You can think and say anything. What matters is **what you are doing to prove it**! What really matters **is what you both say and do, (James 2:17). Both doing and saying is what demonstrates to people and to the YHWH who you are really talking to**!

A Closer Look at the Two Alternatives

One supernatural Being, the Great Dragon, is telling you that you have an immortal soul. How is this promise accomplished? Obviously this question cannot be answered technically. Just think about it from a very high level point of view.

For "The You" to keep on thinking and being aware without a physical brain, then there must be some kind of alternative "cosmic brain" to which "The You" can use after death. The English language is limited in how this idea can be expressed. Please just stay at a high level, and think about what has to be true, to make an immortal soul be true.

In an attempt to make this mind bending "cosmic brain" concept be simplified, so that it can be talked about, consider that essentially the "cosmic brain" concept requires "The You" to keep on thinking and being aware without any kind of a new body to use, because, you have not been given a new body yet.

Remember, that the concept of having an immortal soul has "The You" doing things in Purgatory, or doing things like haunting houses, or finding ways to journey through various gates. All of these things are done while seeking your new body to be whole again. Those who get a new body to use are "in heaven". Otherwise they are somewhere, but still able to think and be aware and do things, but without a body.

Many have groped for words to express this concept of staying alive after death, being able to think and do things on earth with people, and yet "The You" is doing things without any new body yet. Some call this a "**cosmic consciousness**". Essentially, it is "The You" being provided with some kind of "cosmic non-physical body" to use so that you can still do things without having a real new body yet. Regardless of how to express this "**out of body experience**", in order for the Great Dragon to fulfill such a promise, he must have the intelligence, technology, and willingness to somehow provide this "cosmic non-physical body" to you when you die.

The other supernatural Being, the YHWH, is telling you that you do not have an immortal soul. "**His spirit [breath] goes out**, he returns to the ground; **on that very day his thoughts perish**", (Psalm 146:4). This is the same as saying that when your physical body dies, and your physical brain stops working, then "The You" has nothing to use anymore, so that "The You" stops, period. A good list of scriptures on the "**State of the Dead**" can be found at (**www.remnantofgod.org/immortal.htm**).

The Hebrew and Greek Texts use the analogy of "sleeping". When you die, you are essentially asleep, awaiting an awakening in a resurrection, when "The You" is given another new body to use again. Now, think about how the YHWH's promise is accomplished?

Essentially, the promise that "The You" stops thinking when your physical body dies has "The You" suspended from activity for awhile. To suspend "The You", but still be able to recall it back again later, means that "The You" must be saved in some kind of cosmic storage. It might help to think in terms of a vast array of cosmic terabyte disk storage units in heaven, but this is said only to ensure that the concept is understood. This means that the YHWH must have the intelligence, technology, and willingness to somehow record and save "The You", so that later, "The You" can be recalled and given another new body to use again at the resurrection. This concept may be symbolized by **"The Book of Life"**, which has the names of those being saved, (Revelation 20:12).

What all of this means is that "The You" is totally relying upon "your god", either the YHWH or the Great Dragon, to not be lying and to somehow fulfill their promises.

Here is the bottom line: if you are relying upon the Great Dragon, and as a matter of cosmic fact the Great Dragon does not have the intelligence, technology, or willingness to somehow transfer "The You" back into a new body again, **then your fate is total oblivion**. The only way out of this scenario is that **the YHWH has a plan to rescue those confused enough to rely on the Great Dragon**.

Why the Deception Works

The above is not just a complicated philosophical exercise. It can now be understood why the whole world has gone the way of worshipping the Great Dragon. Each of us naturally and intuitively wonders what will happen to us when we die. By agreeing to believe the Great Dragon or one of his priests or agents, that you will not surely die because you have an immortal soul, then the following ramifications are perceived:

1.) You do not have to obey the YHWH, or fear making Him mad. You will keep on living regardless, and you will not be judged by the YHWH, but rather the Great Dragon will eventually make all things right.

2.) Since you do not have to fear making the YHWH mad, it is okay to dismiss the YHWH. This dismissal allows you to be free to choose your own lifestyle and personality. It is by your own will and strength that you decide what is right and wrong "for you". It is by your own will and strength that you will traverse the afterlife's obstacles and gates to get to heaven. Even a living relative can buy you out of a Purgatory or other obstacle. We are talking about living on forever, so then, right now you can decide to be a giving nice guy, or decide to be a selfish bully. Over eternity, and redoing yourself in enough reincarnated "**past lives**", it will all turn out to be the same.

3.) It is to the advantage of the Great Dragon and his agents **to fortify the illusion that the soul is immortal**. That is, to keep "**The Lie**" going, the Great Dragon and his agents will do things to keep people believing that it is true. Making houses "haunted", making apparitions at séances, talking to people from the dead, throwing people in and out of "memories of past lives", and anything else that gives credibility to the belief that the "**Spirits of the Dead**" are still alive, and doing things.

Even the Priesthood of the Great Dragon teaches people to "**be good**". For example, the Egyptian Mysteries teach that you are judged and rewarded differing levels in the afterlife by measuring your conduct against the 42 tests of the Karma, (**http://belsebuub.com/the-42-confessions-from-the-papyrus-of-ani**). Each of these 42 tests asserts that you are essentially "**a good person**". To pass all 42 of them means you are a "**very good person**". Thus, the "good-side" can be understood because people see a path to get a better afterlife, with better rewards. Again, over eternity it will all turn out to be the same.

Thus, we observe that we live in a world filled with both "good" and "evil". **Things happen as each person decides in the moment to either do some good, or to do some bad**. Whatever you decide to do is okay, as your own strength and goodness is the power that will prevail in the afterlife.

In contrast, the YHWH does not let you decide if your own actions are good or bad. Neither does he let a person get away with making "a good show of it". The YHWH decides for Himself. "For the YHWH does not see as man sees; for man looks at the outward appearance, but the YHWH looks at the heart", (1-Samuel 16:7). We must understand which cultural and religious practices the YHWH says are good, and which are not.

The Great Division

In Genesis chapter 3 we are introduced to a created entity talking to Eve, translated into English as "the serpent". This word for "serpent is Strong's Number "**H5175**", and traces back to the concept of "hissing", or a "hisser".

What this means is that the Garden scene may not be talking about a literal snake, but rather a created entity known by its "hissing" characteristics. That is, the entity talking to Eve could well be a created supernatural Being, the Great Dragon, and not just a crawling snake.

In Revelation 20:2 we are told that the ancient serpent is the Devil and is the Adversary, Satan. To be an adversary there must be something that you are opposing. With only a little thought it is apparent that in Genesis 3 the serpent is opposing the idea that Adam and Eve would live forever without experiencing the "Good and Evil" side of self-determination. That is, self determination from the point of view that "I decide what is right and wrong", and, "I decide what is called good and what is called evil". To become the entity that decides these kinds of things, Adam and Eve would have to dismiss the YHWH, and listen to the Great Dragon instead.

The "hisser" only planted the idea that Adam and Eve would still live forever, even if they decide not to listen to the YHWH. Essentially, what the Great Dragon told them was that the dire threat made by the YHWH, that they would indeed die, was not a real threat since they had an immortal soul. Instead of believing the YHWH, they believed the Great Dragon, and decided for themselves which tree was better to eat. The "hisser" did not force them to believe him. They believed him by their own thought processes.

Adam and Eve decided for themselves to disregard the punishment of the YHWH, and proceeded to experience the Tree of "**Good and Evil**". Eve saw that its fruit looked good, that she would become enlightened, and so she decided herself to take and eat. Essentially, they both decided that the YHWH's teachings were wrong, that the "hisser's" teachings were right, and since they would live forever anyway, they no longer needed to fear the YHWH's threat of dying.

Essentially, the great division is about "**Final Authority**". Who are you asking for spiritual enlightenment, help, and instruction? Who is your final Judge in the afterlife, so that He is the one you choose to obey? **Who do you trust with your afterlife experience**?

The Two Priesthoods before the Flood

Many read the account of Cain killing Abel and read right over what is being described. Cain and Abel were each rival High Priests. They both offered the harvest sacrifices to the YHWH on behalf of "their clan". Read again Jude 1:11, 'Woe unto them! For they have gone **in the way of Cain**. . ." Even after the flood, the line of Cain's Priesthood is still a part of the whole story. "Not as Cain, who was of that wicked one, and slew his brother. And wherefore slew he him? **Because his own works were evil, and his brother's righteous**", (1-John 3:12).

This is no minor point: **you can make all of the sacrifices you want, even make them to the YHWH, but if you are not also living as "a righteous person", then your worship does not matter; as your sacrifices are not even recognized**!

That is, **it does not matter who you say you worship. It matters what you are doing in life that shows who you really worship**. Cain was not a righteous person in the eyes of the YHWH. **So his sacrifices, even those made to the YHWH, were not deemed acceptable**.

There are many stories, Myths, which describe the pre-flood battles between the Priesthood of Cain and the Priesthood of Abel (Seth took the place of Abel as High Priest). Diving into these stories is not important for the purposes of this presentation, except to point out that what happened after the Flood was essentially the reestablishment of the same two Priesthoods, the Priesthood of Abel and the Priesthood of Cain.

The Two Priesthoods after the Flood

By keeping only eight people alive through the flood, the male line of Cain's DNA and Priesthood did not survive. Survivors were four males, and their female mates. The DNA line of Cain survived the flood through one of the wives, the wife of Ham.

The Priesthood of Abel, To Noah

Noah was a High Priest of the YHWH after the order of Abel, through Seth. The DNA of Noah followed the ancestry of Seth. The credentials of a High Priest are their priestly garments/robes, and their staff.

This is not a picture of what Noah wore, but can be used to visualize what is meant by "**The Priestly Robes of Noah**".

Noah gave his son Shem his priestly credentials, which he had inherited from Adam, (Mishnah Num. R. iv. 6). In this manner the Priesthood of Abel/Seth was carried over to the other side of the flood. Later, Abraham is born, and there are accounts of his life which include Abraham being trained directly by Shem as a High Priest of the YHWH. In this manner Abraham is counted within the Priesthood of Noah, as a Prophet of the YHWH, (Genesis 20:7).

As told in Genesis, Abraham blessed and transferred his titles and staff to Isaac, and then Isaac blessed and transferred his titles and staff to Jacob.

Aaron's Rod

As a significant missing piece of tracing the Priesthood of Noah, is the story about "**Aaron's Rod**", (**http://en.wikipedia.org/wiki/Aaron%27s_rod**; also Jasher 77:39+). According to Jewish tradition, this rod is essentially a staff providing credentials, **giving the authority to rule the whole world**.

This rod, or staff, was handed down from High Priest to High Priest, and from King to King, starting before the flood with Adam. Adam gave the rod to Seth, Seth onto Noah, to Shem, to Abraham, to Isaac, to Jacob, to Joseph, to Moses, used by Aaron, to Joshua, then onto King David. King David handed the rod down to his descendants, and the Davidic kings used this very same rod as their scepter until the destruction of Solomon's Temple in BC 587.

Since the Temple's destruction this rod has been lost to history. It is assumed to still exist, somewhere. It is anticipated that when the Messiah comes to claim His Kingdom, this same staff will be given to the Messiah as His Scepter (Genesis 49:10), and as His ancestral credentials to rule all of the nations. That is, the credentials to rule the world would then come from Adam down to the Messiah, the second Adam, (1-Corinthians 15:45), who will rule righteously forever after that.

"**Aaron's Rod**" is made of pure crystal sapphire, and weighs about 10.7 pounds. It is in the shape of a trident, having a shaft and three prongs. It is said; "the name of YHWH the Elohim of hosts was engraved thereon", (Jasher 77:39).

This "**Trident Staff**" can be used to visualize what is being talked about as "Aaron's Rod". Pictures of gods holding a Trident can be Noah, Ham, Cush, Nimrod, or Horus.

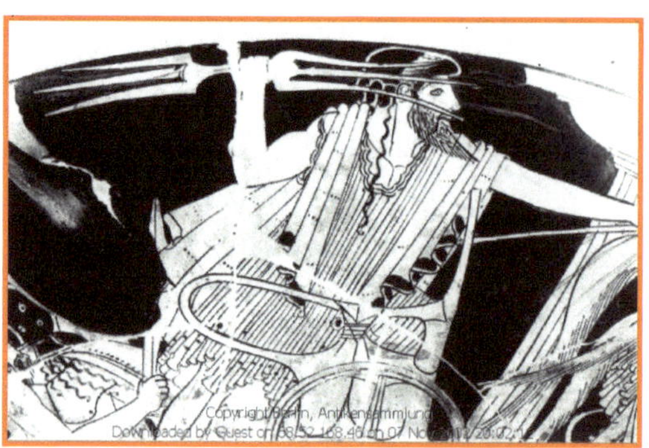

Zeus holding a double-Trident.
Noah's "**Trident Staff**" was never stolen. Cush made a copy.

Neptune (Osiris) holding a "**Trident Staff**".

With the pre-Flood Priestly Robes, and with the crystal sapphire staff from Adam; Noah and Shem were then the post-flood King-Priests of the new world. This line of Priests, this Priesthood, is called the "**Melchizedek Priesthood**", to which Yahoshua the Messiah is the living High Priest. Thus, **Yahoshua is the living King-Priest of the YHWH, having the original authority to rule all nations**.

The Priesthood of Cain, To Cush

Surviving the flood was Noah, three sons, and their wives, (Genesis 9:18). Noah's three sons were Shem, Ham, and Japheth, each son was the King of their own family clan. Each family clan was supposed to migrate in different directions to re-populate the earth.

For this presentation, the important family genealogy to follow is that of Ham. This genealogy is both important and complicated. Much of the complication is that each person has multiple names, found in the differing Myths and languages. Following is an accumulated summary of the numerous Mysteries and Myths, such as Egyptian, Babylonian, Greek, Roman, Hindu, Buddhist, Oriental, and Freemasonry. As it turns out, there are only five major players, gods: Gaia, Cush, Astarte, Nimrod, and Horus.

The Priesthood of Cain was continued after the Flood through Astarte/Rhea, the wife of Cush. Ham could not be a High Priest of the line of Cain because he was a son of Noah, and had no DNA of Cain. Ham's son Cush was the first male born (Genesis 10:6) to have the DNA of Cain, so Cush became the "**Father of the gods**".

Why the Names of the "Gods" Are Confused

Some may be surprised that it is Cush who is the primary god of the Mysteries, the "Ra", and not Nimrod. Ra is Cush, Zeus is Cush, Thoth/Hermes is Cush, and Nimrod is Osiris. As one example of how the differing Mysteries cause confusion, is that Ham is the first "Ra" and King of Egypt, and that Cush took his titles, and so Cush is also "Ra" and King of Egypt too. "When Ra retired from the earth, he appointed Thoth and . . . Thoth became the representation of Ra in the afterlife", (**http://www.bibliotecapleyades.net/thot/esp_thot_9.htm**).

By the transferring of titles and names, Osiris is also "Ra", and so is Horus called "Ra". In the Egyptian Hieroglyphics "Ra" is often prefixed or post fixed with another distinguishing name.

One primary reason for confusion is that the same person has several different names, based not upon who he is, but based upon what he is doing at that time. For example, in the same storyline both Ra and Thoth is actually the same person, but presented with different names. The difference is that his name is "Ra" when he is depicted as doing "Ra" like things, and he is "Thoth" when he is depicted as doing "Thoth" like things, (REF_A: Page 50).

Anubis at the scales is Osiris, doing "Judgment" like things.
Osiris is also on the throne, doing "god of the Underworld" like things.

Another primary reason there is so much confusion is that "father of", "mother of", "son of", "sister of" are often not literal DNA relationships, but are mystical relationships. For example, Isis is said to have a twin sister Nephthys. But Nephthys is actually Isis while doing "Nephthys like things". Nephthys is a mystical sister to Isis. Mystical in the same way that Cush separated himself into multiple gods to "do things", and called them his sons and daughters. This is why genealogy charts of the gods on Wikipedia are so confused. These charts attempt to show DNA lines, when actually the same person is mystically called a son or sister, while doing something else.

What this means is that great confusion is encountered when investigating who is who, because not only do they have different names based upon what they are doing, but also they have different names based upon mystical relationships, which Myth storyline, and which language is telling the story. For such reasons when you are reading about the gods, do not look for names to tell you who they are. Instead look to what they are doing, the symbols around them, their role, their depiction, and their results.

Even so, what emerges is that there are only five primary "gods"; Gaia, Cush, Astarte, Nimrod, and Horus. All of the other gods are lessor-gods. Regardless of the name or the god being addressed, remember that these were real people that lived and then died. In the Mysteries each of these people has their own unique immortal soul that is still alive, and watching.

Being immortal, and being elevated in the afterlife to "the god" level, they can be talked to by men in their earthly prayers. These gods can see who gives offerings to them, and they can do things with crops, animals, people, battles, and love. Thus, in the Mysteries, you are encouraged to ask Osiris for help, because the man Osiris's immortal soul in heaven is alive to hear you, and will do things. In the Mysteries, you are encouraged to ask Isis for help, because the woman Isis' immortal soul in heaven is alive to hear you, and will do things.

In heaven these immortal souls also have new bodies, and thereby each will engage in touch and feel pursuits. Politics, loves, hates, battles, and sexual encounters. Thus, it is understood why there are so many differing Myths and stories about the numerous escapades of the gods.

The Greatest Confusion on Earth

Most understand that language is used to communicate ideas to another person. Equally understood is that far too often the one speaking words is not interpreted correctly by the one hearing those words. We learn little phrases to make this point, such as: "What you think you heard is not what I wanted to say". When it comes to religion, this understanding about language needs to be amplified.

To Whom Are You Talking?

Read this prayer, and ask if you would say "Amen" when it is done?

> "I give praise and blessing unto **God the Father**, the Life and the Light, and the Eternal Good.
> **Holy is God, the Father of all things**, the One who is before the First Beginning.
> Holy is God, whose will is performed and **accomplished by His own Powers**, which He hath given birth to out of Himself.
> [. . .]
> Holy art Thou, who **by Thy Word hast established all things**."

There is a problem with this prayer. If you would say "Amen" to this prayer, you are not being "wrong"; you are being "deceived". This prayer demonstrates what the greatest confusion on earth really is. It is that **even the right sounding words, good words that everyone would think is making a good prayer, does not mean that the prayer is good**.

In this example, **the words sound very good, but in fact they are being directed to someone other than who you think they are**. This is not a prayer to the YHWH. **This is a prayer to the Great Dragon**, recited in one of the Books of Thoth, (REF_C). Here is the beginning part of this prayer:

> "…Poimandres The Great Dragon, who is **The Father -- The Supreme Mind** -- being **Light and Life**, fashioned a glorious **Universal Man** in its **own image**, not an earthy man but a **heavenly Man** dwelling in the **Light of God**. For which cause, with all my soul and all my strength, I give praise and blessing unto **God the Father**…"

The problem is that this prayer **uses the same words** as we would normally expect to hear in a prayer given to the YHWH. We might even hear a reference to the Messiah, as "Thy Word". But these words are directed to another god, the Great Dragon. This demonstrates that **it is not the words that you say; it is to which god you are directing them to**!

From the point of view of worship: the issue is that in a public prayer you may not really know exactly who that prayer is being spoken to. More often than not, you have to admit that you really do not know the person saying the prayer well enough, to know for any certainty who they are talking to. Once, in a public forum, this author witnessed a public prayer to "the Moose Baby", to bless the food. No way! Wrong god! **I did not participate in that**! But most of the time it is not so clear to whom the prayer is being directed. It is easy to be fooled.

The question you have to ask is: "Can you vouch for a certainty that the speaker is not talking to another god, or an agent of the Great Dragon?" For example, in the opening sentence, did he say "**Our heavenly Father**"? Well, this prayer from the Book of Thoth demonstrates that the title "**God the Father**" can refer to the Great Dragon, and not only to the YHWH. Therefore, just opening a prayer with "**Our heavenly Father**" is not enough information for you to assume to know which god is being praised.

Take this to an extreme, to ensure making the point.
If the person giving the public prayer is a self-professed witch doctor, so that you know for a certainty that he is talking to the Great Dragon or one of his agents, and you hear him say: "We give praise and blessing unto **God the Father**, …", would you then say "Amen"?

Think about it, you really should not. Why? Because even though you can play a game inside of your own mind, and redirect those words to mean what you think they should mean, so that the prayer is reworded and then redirected to the YHWH, in your own mind, your public "Amen" is an acknowledgement to all that hear you that you agree with that person's public prayer going to the Great Dragon. Do you really agree to pray to the Great Dragon? Thus, you really should not be saying "Amen".

But the problem is not in seeing through the extreme cases. The problem is in seeing through the typical cases. The witch doctor giving a public prayer is not the problem. The problem is when a typical person gives a typical prayer. Because the question you must ask yourself is exactly the same. **To which "god" is that person really talking to**?

You cannot just use titles or slogans to tell the difference between the two supernatural Beings. For example, Thoth's center of worship was at Khmunu (Hermopolis) in Upper Egypt, where he was worshipped as "**The Creator God**". But the YHWH is also "**The Creator God**", (Genesis 2). This means that you cannot use this title, "**Creator God**", to automatically distinguish between them. If someone opens a prayer to "**The Creator God**", you do not necessarily know to which "**Creator God**" they are talking.

It is even worse than this! As a fact, the letters "YHWH" (יהוה) are very commonly seen as **Occult and Gnostics symbols**. The Occult and Gnostic Shamans often use the name of God, "YHWH", in casting spells and healing, as did the ancient Egyptians:

> "for that others (pagans) use the words '**the God of Abraham**' when they are **driving out devils**. And again the Egyptians use in their rites, from which they promise wonderful effects, the names of '**Abraham, Isaac, Jacob, and Israel**'. Also (iv. 33) Origen mentions the use of the form '**The God of Abraham, the God of Isaac, the God of Jacob**' in incantations, and that the same is often to be met within books of Magic. He adds that the formula '**The God of Abraham, the God of Isaac, who didst overwhelm the Egyptians and the King of the Egyptians in the Red Sea**,' was in common use against demons and the Powers of Evil",
> (**http://www.sacred-texts.com/gno/gar/gar44.htm**).

It is manifest that these incantations, spells, and magical phrases are not being directed to the YHWH, who requires devotion and obedience along with prayers. These words "sound very good"; you may even say these same words too. **But it is not what you say**; it is to **which supernatural Being or agent you are talking to**. After all, **who is listening so as to grant those magical requests**?

The Great Dragon also has these titles:
"**The Universal Life**", "**The Mind of the Universe**",
"**The Creative Intelligence**", "**The Absolute Emperor**",
"**The Divine Mind**".

You may have heard some of these titles in public prayers, especially those prayers given to open meetings and at graduations. **Did you say "Amen"**?

What Do Your Words Mean?

There is more confusion. It is not only which "god" you are talking to, it is also a matter of what are the definitions of those words being used. We all know this. Why is it that during a prayer we forget, and assume their words means the same as whatever we think they should mean?

As one example, a quote from the Catholic Church:

> "The Catholic Church does not recognize Mormon baptism as valid because, although Mormons and Catholics **use the same words**, those **words have completely unrelated meanings** for each religion", (**http://www.catholic.com/quickquestions**).

Talking about the Mormons is not the point. The point is that many religions use the exact same words, **but in reality those words have very different meanings**, and thereby the exact same sentence, word for word, does not mean the same thing. It is not a matter that people do not understand this to be true. It is a matter that **they forget that it is vitally important to remember that it is true**.

In religion this means that a public prayer not only changes "**purpose**" based on **to which god it is being directed**, but it also changes "**meaning**" based on **what those words mean** to the person saying them. Those same words will mean one thing to you listening, but something entirely different to the one speaking. In a public prayer, **what matters is what those words mean to the one speaking. Those are the words being tossed into the air for some deity to hear**. If you do not know for sure what the speaker means by his words, then you may not want to say "Amen".

Demonstrating the Depth of the Confusion

Not only is it important to know to which god a person is talking, and not only is it important to know the definitions of the words he is speaking, it is also important to know which god they try to obey. **The question of "To whom do you obey?" is the third and the hardest aspect of the great confusion**.

Many have seen the "Star Wars" movies, or at least been exposed to the phrases the "**Good Side of the Force**" versus the "**Dark Side of the Force**". Even in these movies we are all told to follow the "**Good Side of the Force**". This goal, to be "**a good person**", is not made up:

> "A distinction [in Babylon] was made between good serpents and bad serpents, one kind being represented as the serpent of 'Agathodaemon', or the good divinity, another as the serpent of 'Cacodaemon', or the evil one . . . In Egypt, the 'Uraeus', or the 'Cerastes', was the good serpent, the 'Apophis' the evil one", (REF_B: Page 220).

There is much more depth to this than merely asking if someone is "**a good person**". You can be "**a good person**" and not be worshipping the YHWH. You can be "**a good person**" and worship the "**Good Serpent**" too.

In the Egyptian Mysteries it is believed that during life one had to fulfill a list of cosmic laws. These laws were a series of affirmations called the "**42 Negative Confessions**". It is taught that a person is judged at death by how well they did relative to these 42 tests of Karma. When these 42 tests are read it is understood that the Egyptian Mysteries expect people to **be good people**, not evil people. These tests intend to measure how good a person was. The good person passes cosmic gates and goes on to heaven, and the bad person goes some place else (reincarnation).

"The 42 tests of Karma are confessions:

1. Hail. . . I have not committed sin.
2. Hail. . . I have not robbed with violence.
3. Hail. . . I have done no violence.
4. Hail. . . I have not stolen.
5. Hail. . . I have not slain men.
6. Hail. . . I have not made light the bushel.
7. Hail. . . I have not acted deceitfully.
8. Hail. . . I have not stolen the property of the god.
9. Hail. . . I have not told lies. [the list goes on for tests 10-42]"

(**http://belsebuub.com/the-42-confessions-from-the-papyrus-of-ani**).

In the Egyptian Mysteries the person who had done well in life will pass on to heaven. The person who had done very well in life will pass on to heaven as a new god. For example, it is said that Osiris did very well, so he is now a god in heaven, and listens to the prayers of men.

The point is, even in the Mysteries a person is taught to do good deeds, and to be "**a good person**". Also in the Hebrew and Greek Texts a person is taught to do good deeds, and to be "**a good person**". Further, many people do not have any religious tendency at all, yet they too can be "**a good person**". Thus, **you cannot tell which supernatural Being a person tries to obey, by just determining that they are "a good person"**.

Consider: you meet a man that can do very well in the 42 tests of Karma. This man is "**a good person**", as he does not steal, he does 'this' right, and he does 'that' well. But, when that same "**good person**" gives the prayer recited above, given to praise the Great Dragon, is it now okay to say "Amen"? The fact is that just because they are "**a good person**" does not change the direction of their prayer, or the definitions of their words. You still may not want to say "Amen".

What all this means is that just being "**a good person**" is not definitive enough to demonstrate to whom you give your obedience. For this very reason each supernatural Being, the YHWH and the Great Dragon, **has their own list of key laws of obedience, unique to their side of the Priesthood**. This presentation is calling these key laws the "**Specific Laws**" which immediately demonstrate which supernatural Being you are obeying. Both rival Priesthoods teach you how to be "**a good person**". **But it is the obedience to the "Specific Laws" which clearly delineate which supernatural Being you are really worshipping**.

Short List of "Specific Laws"

Each Supernatural Being has a "short list" of delineating "**Specific Laws**". Categorizing the 42 tests of Karma demonstrates that these tests for being "**a good person**" are much generalized, not very specific, and almost ambiguous. But each supernatural Being has listed some very "**Specific Laws**", and **teaches people to do these things as proof of their devotion to "Me", in contrast to "Him"**. With only a little thought you can start to itemize a "short list" of some obvious "**Specific Laws**".

The Priesthood of Noah	The Priesthood of Cush
Exodus 31:12-17: Worship the YHWH on the Seventh Day. That is, worship Me on My Day, the Day that I say.	Worship "god" on the Day of the Sun. That is, worship Me on My Day, the Day that I say.
Leviticus 23: Keep the Holy Days of the YHWH. That is, worship Me on My Days as I say.	Keep the Holy Days of "the Church", or those of your "religion". The Days which were anciently the same Holy Days dedicated to one of the primary gods. That is, worship Me on My Days as I say.
Leviticus 11: Learn to discern the Holy versus the Profane by staying pure and eating only "Clean Meats". That is, worship Me in this specific manner as I say.	No attempt to staying pure, eat anything. That is, worship Me in this specific manner as I say.
Leviticus 18:1-5, Deut. 12:30-31: Do not do as you did in Egypt… but do these things that I say to do…	Do whatever things your "Church" or your "religion" says to do. Follow your own "heart".
Priests do not mark worshippers with symbols on their bodies.	Priests routinely mark worshippers with symbols on their bodies, especially on the "**Third Eye**".
(The list of "**Specific Laws**" making distinct contrast continues.)	(The list of "**Specific Laws**" making distinct contrast continues.)

It is All about Definitions of Words

The definitions of words are vital. This point can be demonstrated by looking at 1-Corinthians 12:3: "and that no man can say that **Jesus is the Lord**, but by the Holy Ghost". The problem with this verse is that people can say it, and mean it, but they do not even have to be a "Christian" to do so. The other religions recognize that Jesus lived, and was a prophet, and started his own religion. People can say "**Jesus is Lord**", because it is open to definitions as to "**Lord of what**?"

People may ask you "Do you know **The Lord Jesus**?" You will hear this question, and quickly apply your own definitions to those words, and may then quickly answer "Yes". But to which "**Lord**" and to which "**Jesus**" did they ask you about? After all, your "Yes" answer often leads them to ask you to join them in some religious ceremony. It is easy to be fooled.

Do they mean that "**Lord**" which has his day of worship on "**The Lord's Day**", that is on Sun-Day? Well, that would be the "**Baal's Day**", as "Baal" means "Lord". Are you saying "**Yes**" because "**Baal**" is your "**Lord**"? **Perhaps confessing that Yahoshua (Jesus) is "Lord" means something significantly different**?

Do they mean that "**Jesus**" who tells them that the YHWH has changed his mind, and that he has dismissed the "**Specific Laws**" of the YHWH, now calling them "**old**"?

Do they mean that "**Jesus**" who tells them is it now okay to eat anything they want, and to just be "**a good person**" by doing whatever "**The Church**" or "**Karma**" tells them to do?

Do they mean that "**Jesus**" who tells them to be pious by keeping the Christmas (Bacchus) and Easter (Ishtar) festivals condemned by the YHWH?

Do they mean that "**Jesus**" who tells them they are saved by god's unconditional grace, even when they dismiss the YHWH?

> "Little children, **let no one deceive you**: The one who **practices righteousness** [verb] is **righteous** [noun]", (1-John 3:7).

This point is demonstrated because it is **the definitions of words** that completely change the meaning of the question, and what is actually being asked. You cannot assume that those words mean the same thing to them, as they do to you. Just saying "Yes" may not be the right answer.

From this point of view, it can be understood why the YHWH tells us that He is a **jealous** Elohim/God. From His point of view we are His kids, and He wants to be our Dad. As parents we can understand that naturally He wants us to listen to Him, and ask Him for help and instruction. It is a very painful experience to watch one of your own kids turn away from you, and seek out someone else to be their Dad (parent) instead. **The definitions of our words start with the Hebrew/Aramaic Text of our Dad, the YHWH**.

A Note on Differences in Administration

We observe that many people try to show their obedience to the YHWH by keeping His list of "**Specific Laws**". And it is important to observe that most of these people practice these laws in differing ways. For example, some people will keep the Sabbath "this way", and some people will keep the Sabbath "that way". This is also true with differences on which Calendar to use for Holy Days.

In making decisions about the details, we do it "this way", and we do it "that way", we are effectively making judgments about how the law is administrated within "our circle". All sides of the debates about how to keep the Sabbath are still doing so within the framework of wanting to show obedience to the YHWH by keeping His list of "**Specific Laws**", and not the alternative "**Specific Laws**". **There will be differences in Administration, 1-Corinthians 12:28, so do not fight the diversity, enjoy the diversity**.

Just How Deep Does This Confusion Go?

If only things were simple, and everything was "black and white". We probably can understand the importance of **knowing which god a person is talking to**. We probably can understand the importance of **knowing the definitions of the words** a person is using. And we probably can understand the importance of **knowing which god they are trying to obey**. We probably can even understand that:

> "**The Lie**" of the Great Dragon is his promising you that you are a composite of two parts, "a Physical Body and a Spiritual Mind", two separate things, wherein your "**Mind**" is immortal, and that your "**Body**" is mortal. Your afterlife will be **immortality in a new spiritual Body**, even when you **dismiss the YHWH as if He is not needed to bring it about**.

With all of this probably being understood, **what we observe** is that most of the people we know **believe in some kind of a confused mixture** of all of these. For example, we observe people who try to obey the YHWH by keeping His Sabbaths, but at the same time they believe they have an immortal soul. We observe people who do not believe they have an immortal soul, but yet worship on the Sun's Day specific to the other Priesthood.

In the arena of definitions of words, there seems to be hundreds of hotly debated meanings of the numerous "key words" that are used to form religious doctrines. As a matter of fact, **we observe that "everything" seems to be "completely confused"**!

Most of this great confusion can be clarified by better understanding what the Mysteries teach. If we know what the Mysteries teach, and what they tell us to do as their "**Specific Laws**" of worship, then we can better discern when we see something that is just not right.

Certainly we need to be able to discern those religious practices that are "**Specific Laws**" to worshipping the YHWH, versus those religious practices that are "**Specific Laws**" to worshipping the Great Dragon. **The goal of The Great Dragon is to deceive people so that they either wind up in oblivion, or fail to reach their full potential**. To help in clarifying much of the confusion, the following details about the Mysteries are presented.

The Foundational Stories of The Mysteries

The following is a composite storyline taken from various Mysteries and Myths, such as Egyptian, Babylonian, Greek, Roman, Hindu, Buddhist, Oriental, and Freemasonry. Each Mystery tells different stories about the same "gods", and in their own language, so that each god has several different names. Regardless of the storyline variances, these Mysteries and their Myths basically follow the same theme.

The Mystery's "Gods"

There are only five primary "gods": Gaia, Cush, Astarte, Nimrod, and Horus. **These were real people, which lived and died**. Because of "**The Lie**" of the Great Dragon, it is taught that these people's immortal souls lived on after death, **having full memory, personality, and awareness** as they had before death. Each of these gods is seen as a different star in the night sky. For example, Osiris is the man of the constellation Orion, (REF_B: Page 15), and is the "Dog Star", Sirius, in the constellation of "Canis Major", (**http://en.wikipedia.org/wiki/Sirius**). Each of these gods is associated with different planets, symbols, and character traits.

When verifying the information contained herein, Wikipedia is a great source to start. Remember that each of these gods have different names in each language, have more than one name based on what they are doing at the time of the story or the picture presented, and most confusing of all, they inherited the same names, titles, wives, and symbols from their fathers. That is, they became what their father was, plus what they became. What is presented herein is the composite view, keeping track of the players after putting the numerous stories and Myths together.

Cush Is the Top "God" of the Mysteries

The reason why Ham is not really a major god, as far as this presentation is concerned, is that Ham starts out as Ra/Zeus, and was the first "**Father of the gods**", until his children grew up. Ham literally ate his own male children to avoid anyone taking his place, (REF_B: Page 70, 208). But eventually Ham was completely usurped by Cush, and then Cush became Ra/Zeus, and everything else Ham used to be. There are stories/Myths which have both Ham and Cush doing things together. But later Cush forcibly took the credentials and Kingship from Ham, as well as all of his titles, names, symbols, wives, and properties.

By understanding the different names of the gods, Bible verses such as Isaiah 46:1 can be better understood:

> (quoting word-for-word) "...has bowed **Bel** [and] stoops **Nebo** [they are], their idols for the beast and for the cattle...". "**Bel**" is Cush as "**The Confounder**", as in mixing it up. "**Nebo**" is Hebrew for "**Nabu**", and is Cush as **Mercury**, (**http://en.wikipedia.org/wiki/Nabu**).

Remember that the same god has different names based upon what he is doing, or his representative role. Capturing the context in chapter 45, Israel is finally triumphant. In that scene the top god "**Cush the Confounder**" will bow down. **Mercury** is Cush is the representative god of the "**Serpent's Wisdom**" and his Priesthood. Thus, Cush stoops low before the YHWH and Israel. With their rival Priesthood idols being tossed to the animals, the entire religious system, represented by Cush and the other gods of the Mysteries, are subdued. That is, **a complete religious victory**.

The First Battles between the Two Priesthoods

There are many storylines and Myths describing the first battles between the Priesthood line of Noah and Shem, against the Priesthood line of Cush, Nimrod, Astarte, and Ninus. Following is a simplified and short version of a composite view, (REF_B: Page 163).

Right after the Flood, Noah had carried over the credentials of the YHWH's Priesthood, and essentially ruled the world of only a small band of his descendants. Over time Ham's family started to separate from Noah and his authority.

Cush represented the first male child after the Flood which had the DNA of Cain. Thus, Cush had the bloodline credentials to restart the Priesthood of Cain on the post-side of the Flood.

Ham stole the Priesthood robes from Noah and hid them for Cush. But neither Ham nor Cush could steal the Trident shaped rod (staff) of Adam. Cush duplicated Noah's "**Trident Staff**", and then literally restarted the Priesthood of the Great Dragon of Cain again. The primary symbol for this Priesthood became the "**Serpent**", which is seen somewhere within most pictures and statues of "the gods".

After Cush's son Nimrod came of age, Ham, Cush, and Nimrod threw lots to decide who would rule what. That is, who would rule over the Heaven, or over the Earth, or over the Sea. The lots fell so that Ham ruled the Heavenly abodes (cities), and Cush ruled the Earth (plains), and Nimrod ruled the Sea. The Sea is also called the Underworld, or the **Abyss**.

The ancient meaning of "**Heaven**" is not talking about outer space or ethereal cities in the sky. The Heavens represented the cities in the higher mountains, the lofty heights in the clouds. This is why you can read stories about men making a journey to Heaven, and return. Ham was the god of the Heavenly cities. The Earth represented the cities on the plains, and the Sea represented the oceans, waterways, and islands.

What this split in dominion did, was to add three more credentials for rulership to be coveted. Eventually, Cush forcibly took everything from his father Ham. Cush "inherited" all of Ham's titles, names, properties, wives, and servants. This included the title of being the "**god of Heaven**". Thus, Cush became the "**god of Heaven and Earth**". Cush's son Nimrod remained the "**god of the Sea/Underworld**". Later, Cush gave Nimrod his own titles and names. Cush then took a "back seat"; allowing Nimrod to rule all three zones, as the "**god of Heaven and Earth and the Underworld**", while Cush remained the High Priest of the Great Dragon's Priesthood.

Noah still had the Trident rod of Adam, the credential of world rulership, and so repeatedly warned Nimrod to stop claiming his conflicting authority. Eventually Noah's son Shem (Set) gathered an army, pursued Nimrod, and executed him. Shem then cut Nimrod's dead body into many pieces, and sent each piece to a different community as a warning not to follow the line of Cain. The rest of this part of the story is continued below, but the net result is that a successor to the executed Nimrod (Osiris) was born, the god Horus.

Eventually, Horus grew up and again challenged the authority of Shem. This time Shem fought Horus in a one-on-one duel. Those watching the duel judged that Shem lost the fight. Shem was severely pierced, but lived. Horus lost one eye. This lost eye is the "Eye of Ra", or the "Eye of Horus", or the "**All Seeing Eye**", that is seen on our one dollar bills.

The Virgin Birth and Sun-Day Worship

Attending worship services on Sunday did not begin with the advent of Christianity. Sunday, the first (in rank) day of the week, has been a religious day of worship throughout history. The practice of worshipping god on the day of the Sun was intentionally used to distinguish those who worshipped "the gods" of the Mysteries, in contrast to those who worshipped the YHWH on the seventh day of His Creation week. **<u>This contrast, as to which day is the day to worship the supernatural Being of your choice, is not an accident</u>**. It is a "**Specific Law**" used to distinguish which of the two supernatural Beings you are worshipping.

The Seven Days of the Week

The first thing to understand is that the order of the seven days of the week is not random. Sunday is the first day of the week from the point of view of being the highest in rank. Each day of the week is associated with a planet, and they are assigned an order on purpose. Each planet is ruled by a male and a female god. Look carefully at this ancient Egyptian depiction.

A "**Karmic Wheel**" from Egypt.

Those symbols represent planets. Notice the three faded pyramids: Saturn (brightest), Moon (taller), Jupiter (reddish). By following the connecting lines between the seven planets, the order of the week days is given:

The Sun is at the top, which is Sunday, the first day of the week.
The Moon is connected next, Monday.
Then Mars is connected, Tuesday.
Then Mercury is connected, Wednesday.
Then Jupiter is connected, Thursday.
Then Venus is connected, Friday
Then Saturn is connected, Saturday.

Thus, we see a pyramid of planets, or days of the week as follows:

Sunday, The **Sun**
Saturday, **Saturn** Monday, The **Moon**
Friday, **Venus** Tuesday, **Mars**
Thursday, **Jupiter** Wednesday, **Mercury**

The Day of the Sun being first and at the top of the pyramid is no accident. **It is a focal tenet of the Mysteries to worship god on the Day of the Sun**. As demonstrated later, **the "Seven Heads" of "The Beast" of Revelation 13 is directly related to the seven days of the week, that is, to the seven planets and the deities that rule over them.**

The Birth of the "Incarnate God", Horus

The alternative worship system, generically being called "**The Mysteries**", began about 4600 years ago. Ham stole the Priesthood robes from Noah and hid them for Cush, (Jasher 7:27; **http://bhporter.com/Stolen%20Garment.htm**). Later, Nimrod received the Priesthood/Kingship authority from Cush, who thereafter stayed in the background as the High Priest, while his son ruled. Thus, both Cush and Nimrod/Osiris is a "Ra", the god of the first ranked planet, the sun.

Nimrod (Osiris) was the first man after the Flood to survive Ham eating his grandkids. Nimrod had the DNA credentials of the pre-Flood Cain, and obtained the titles of being the "**god of Heaven and Earth and Sea**". Thus, Nimrod claimed the full measure of the Priesthood of Cain. That is, he became the "**God of Heaven and Earth and the Underworld**". It is Nimrod, as Osiris, which is the "**Judge of the Dead**", and Nimrod decides who goes to heaven, and who goes someplace else.

Astarte/Ishtar/Isis was Nimrod's mother, and his sister, and also his wife.

The Priesthood line of Cush and Nimrod was a deliberate rebellion against the YHWH, who had His own Priesthood line of authority through Noah and his son Shem. Because of the Dead Sea Scrolls it is known that Noah and Shem started the now called, "**Melchizedek Priesthood**" of the YHWH. This is the Priesthood line to which the resurrected and exalted Yahoshua the Messiah is now the living High Priest, (Hebrews 8:1). Thus, throughout the centuries the YHWH has always had His own Priesthood line, and branches, promoting His precepts and "**Specific Laws**", **way before Moses was even born**.

Shem, upon hearing of Nimrod/Osiris' rival activities and after repeated warnings, gathered an army and sought to capture Osiris. Osiris fled, but was eventually captured and executed for his rebellion. There is a suggestion that Osiris's capture and execution was in a cave, in what is now Rome. The execution included the cutting-up of Osiris' dead body into many pieces. Each piece was sent to a specific region of the world as proof of Osiris' death, and as a warning against following his rebellious Priesthood authority.

Astarte/Isis, upon hearing of the death of her son-brother-husband, wailed loudly for him. Many are familiar with the religious customs surrounding the "**Wailing for Tammuz**", (Ezekiel 8:14).

Astarte then journeyed and sought after the scattered cut-up pieces of Osiris. Eventually she gathered each piece of Osiris, except the phallus, and with the help of Cush/Thoth reconstructed Osiris' dead body long enough to perform a secret magic ceremony.

In this secret ceremony Astarte/Isis and Thoth used the gathered body parts of Osiris to perform a very unique ceremony and séance. This ceremony somehow allowed Osiris' after death heavenly living '**immortal soul body**' to impregnate Astarte. In this manner she thereby conceived "**The Incarnated Son of God**", and did so as a "**Virgin Mother**".

Thus, it is taught that Astarte bore Osiris' "**Only Begotten Son**", calling him Horus. That is, it is said that Osiris's own sperm magically came from Osiris's after death glorified '**immortal soul body**', so therefore, Horus is Osiris' **only Son ever to be begotten by an after death 'immortal soul body**'. The Mysteries teach that Horus is the only one ever conceived from such an after death '**immortal soul body**', so that Horus is literally said to be the "**<u>Only Begotten Son of God</u>**",
(**http://en.wikipedia.org/wiki/Osiris_myth**) and
(**www.taroticallyspeaking.com/knowledge/the-story-of-isis-and-osiris**).

The descendants of Horus became the Kings and dynasties of various city-states. Osiris is the "**Father of the gods**"; in that Osiris fathered Horus, who then fathered the god/kings that were granted the rulership over the nations.

A problem was that everyone knew that Osiris was long dead. As proof that the child Horus was in fact "**The Incarnated Son of Osiris**", from Osiris himself, Astarte and the other priests claimed that they witnessed an evergreen branch grow out of a dead log, in one night.

This miracle happened the same day the child Horus was born, which was on the day of the winter solstice. In the timeframe of Alexander the Great who conquered Persia circa BC 331, the Chaldean and Greek Mysteries shared stories. Circa BC 331 the winter solstice occurred on <u>December 25th</u>, as reckoned by the original Julian calendar which the Romans would later use. Thus, Christmas is on December 25th, as decreed by the Papal System in Rome. This evergreen branch is the modern "**Christmas Yule-log**" or "**Christmas Tree**" we know today.

Later, Astarte was deified as "**The Virgin Mother**", and "**The Queen of Heaven**". The well known "**Madonna and Child**" theme, "**The Virgin Mother and Child**", is very common to nearly all religions. Thus, the first "**Mother and Child**" nativity story began over 4600 years ago, which is about 2600 years before Yahoshua the Messiah was even born.

It is expected that the reader will perceive numerous parallels, in both storyline and titles, with those found in Christianity regarding the "**Virgin Birth**" and the "**Only Begotten Son of God**". Ancient people already knew these "Christmas" stories from the Mysteries.

Today, archaeologists find remains of temples and idols all over the world having the same "**Madonna and Child**" religious theme. The common theme is "**The Triune God**", with "**Three Persons**" being worshipped as "**One God**". The most common is "**The Father and the Mother and the Child**", being worshipped as "**One God**". This common theme is not about Mary the mother of Yahoshua. This common theme is about Astarte, the Priestess who orchestrated the whole storyline. The Christian "**Father, Son, and Holy Ghost**" "**Triune God**", started out as the "**Osiris, Horus, and Isis**" "**Triune God**". In the Mysteries there are many combinations of male and female "**Triune Gods**". Some "**Triune Gods**" are one male with two females, but always as "**Three Persons**" being worshipped as "**One God**".
(**http://en.wikipedia.org/wiki/Triple_deity**).

Hindu Vasudeva taking away Krishna from Devaki

In Egypt the "**Mother and Child**" was worshipped under the names of "**Isis and Horus**". In India they are worshipped as "**Isi and Iswara**". In Asia they were worshipped as "**Cybele and Deoius**". In Rome they were worshipped as "**Fortuna and Jupiter-puer**", Jupiter the boy. Other eastern religions worshipped the "**Great Goddess Mother**". In Greece as Ceres the "**Great**

Mother" with "**the Babe**" at her breast. They were worshipped as **Irene** the "**Goddess of Peace**" and the boy "**Plutus**". In the Orient the Jesuit missionaries were astonished to find the counterpart of the "Madonna and Child" being worshipped as Shing Moo, "**The Holy Mother**" and "**the child in her arms**", (REF_B: Page 21).

Horus is not the only one said to be born as an "**Incarnate God**" through a miraculous conception. So too are "**Christna**", "**Prometheus**", "**Esculapius**", "**Wittoba**", and "**Buddha**" said to be miraculously born as an "**Incarnate God**". <u>The Mysteries have a common theme of worshipping a "**Triune God**"</u> as if it were "**One God**", wherein one member is an "**Incarnate God**".

The Lord's Day, Sunday

Often in the Hebrew Text the Israelites are severely chastised for worshipping "**The Lord**". The Hebrew for "Lord" is the word "**Baal**", and is often expressing a plural meaning. That is, they were chastised for worshipping "**The Lords**" of Egypt and Babylon, the gods of the Mysteries. When they turned away to worship Baal, the first thing that they did was to switch the day of worship, from the Sabbath of the YHWH, to worshipping Baal on Sunday, (REF_B: Page 22).

The Egyptian Mysteries teach that the god Osiris is represented as "The Sun", which rises each morning to enlighten the world. With only a short investigation it is manifest that "**The Lord**", Baal, is Nimrod/Belus (REF_B: Page 27). Those who worship "**The Lord**", worship Osiris on his day of the week, "**The Lord's Day**", that is, on Sun - Day.

("From Sabbath to Sunday", by Samuele Bacchiocchi, 1977), and
("Truth Triumphant, The Church In The Wilderness", by Benjamin George Wilkinson, PH. D., 1997, Sabbath Churches in history all around the world).

Thus, the practice of Sunday Worship **is in deliberate opposition** to that of resting and worshipping the YHWH on His Day of the week, the Sabbath Day, Saturday.

Yahoshua the Messiah declared to all that He was in full agreement with the practice of keeping this "**Specific Law**", as Yahoshua affirmed that the Sabbath was also His day, by stating that He is "**The Lord of the Sabbath Day**", (Matthew 12:8). It becomes manifest that the followers of the Messiah would worship the YHWH on that day in which Yahoshua said that He is its Lord, "**The Sabbath Day**".

The Seven Heads of The Beast

"**The Beast with Seven Heads**" has been known throughout history, and has been the alternative worship system since Adam and Eve. Thus, worshipping "**The Beast**" and taking "**The Mark of the Beast**" has been a choice throughout the centuries. The Text in Revelation warning about taking "**The Mark of the Beast**" has been germane to all who have ever lived, not just for a few believers in the future.

Irenaeus writing "Against Heresies, Book V" circa AD 175 is **very clear** that the original Greek Text written by the Apostle John spelled out the number '666', and did not use the three-Greek characters, as are found in later copies.

> "John [The Apostle] says further: ". . . , unless he who has the mark of the name of the beast or the number of his name; and the number is six hundred and sixty-six," that is, **six times a hundred, six times ten, and six units**. [He gives this] **as a summing up of the whole of that apostasy which has taken place during six thousand years**."
> **(www.earlychristianwritings.com/text/irenaeus-book5.html)**

That is, John wrote:

ἐξ ακόσιοι	ἐξ ήκοντα	ἕξ ,
six hundreds	six tens	six.

Sumerian Relief: a "**Beast with Seven Heads**", with one head wounded.

Hindu: Vishnu, Brahma, Shiva / Maheshwara (Horus)

This image needs to be studied. Notice the Serpent is coming out of the sea, and the "Seven Heads" above Brahma's (Cush) crown. Notice the "**Trident Staff**" passed to Shiva (Horus).

Table of the Seven Heads of the Beast

Worshipping "**The Beast**" is the lifestyle which follows one of the seven "**Schools of Thought**" of the Great Dragon. **The "Seven Heads" of "The Beast" of Revelation 13 is directly related to the seven days of the week, that is, to the seven planets and the deities they represent.** The Day of the Sun being first and at the top of the pyramid is no accident. **Worshipping the Great Dragon on the Day of the Sun is one of his "Specific Laws"**.

Each Head is a unique Branch, a "**School of Thought**", a Priesthood or Hierarchical System of the Great Dragon. There are **three symbols** which are universally found in each of these seven "**Schools of Thought**": "**The Cross**", "**The All Seeing Eye**", and "**The Serpent**".

			The Sun Sunday **Cush as Thoth** **Astrology / New Age System**			
		Saturn Saturday **Osiris** The Male side **Freemason System**		The Moon Monday **Ishtar** The Female side **Papal System**		
	Venus Friday **Isis** **Hinduism, System**				Mars Tuesday **Bacchus** **Military, Nobility, Caste System**	
Jupiter Thursday **Cush as Thoth** **Buddhism, Humanism System**						Mercury Wednesday Cush as Nebo, as Ninus **Shaman System**

Sunday: The Sun, Cush, the Great Dragon

One of the titles of the Great Dragon is the "**Supreme Being**". Sunday is the day of worship to the "**Supreme Being**". The High Priest and messenger of the Great Dragon was **Cush**. Cush talked directly to the Great Dragon, and passed that information onto others in "**Sacred Scrolls**". It is said that Cush, depicted as Thoth, wrote over 20,000 "**Sacred Scrolls**", of which only a very few have been found.

This Head of the Beast is the "**Astrology and New Age**" System, which is the supernatural hierarchal system of "**Spiritual Enlightenment**". This includes the worship of the "**Host of Heaven**", which are the seven planets as they traverse the Zodiac and influence daily events. In this system, worshippers are encouraged to contact and talk directly with one or more "**Supernatural Spirit Guides**". The "**Supernatural Spirit Guides**" have a hierarchy, with the "**Spirit Masters**" at the top. Through this hierarchy different people claim higher levels of "**Spiritual Enlightenment**", thus creating a man-made Priesthood hierarchy too.

One of the symbols representing the weekday pyramid is a pyramid without having the topmost corner stone present. As a commonly seen example, on the dollar bill is a pyramid without the topmost corner stone present. Instead there is the "**All Seeing Eye**", or the "**Eye of Providence**" detached from the pyramid, but obviously is intended to be attached to it.

The "**All Seeing Eye**", the "**Eye of Horus**",
is the "**Spiritual Enlightenment**" through Cush.

This missing corner piece represents the Great Dragon as the "**Hidden One**". This is the god that is really being worshipped, through his various Priesthoods and agents. This will become more evident after reading through the other weekdays.

Thus, the "**Spiritual Enlightenment**", often called the "**New Age Movement**", is just another "**School of Thought**", just another Head of the Beast, worshipping the Great Dragon through his "**Spirit Guides**" Priesthood and agents.

Monday: The Moon, Ishtar

Each of the planets has both a male side and a female side, both a male and female god representation. The Moon has both Cush and Ishtar as its representatives. That is, both Cush and Ishtar have the Moon as one of their primary symbols.

The right side of the weekday pyramid, Monday, Tuesday, Wednesday, has its focus on **Ishtar**. That is, from the female point of view, how do "things" relate to Ishtar? Monday represents Ishtar herself. In this weekday governed by the female side, the men (Priests) cannot have sex with women; and the women (Priestesses) cannot have sex with men.

This Head of the Seven Headed Beast **is the Papal System**, which mostly follow the Chaldean Mysteries, but changing the words to sound more "Christian". The Papal System has also incorporated several key aspects of the Egyptian Mysteries as well.

In the Chaldean Mysteries Ishtar is the dominant female god. Ishtar is the "**Queen of Heaven**", the "**Mother of God**" and the "**Virgin Mother**". The "**Triune God**" is Bacchus, Ishtar, and Ninus, with Ninus called Tammuz when referring to "**Bacchus Incarnate**".

In Revelation 13 it states that one of the seven heads appeared to have been killed, but was healed. The Chaldean Mysteries is that wounded head. Bacchus (Osiris) was executed for rebellion. But his Priesthood and Scepter line lives on; because Ishtar (Isis) gave miraculous birth to Ninus (Horus). Through the "**Triune God**" and "**Savior Horus**", the Chaldean Mysteries and "right to rule" Scepter line lives on.

Revelation 2:12-13 has the throne, or seat, of Satan in Pergamos. In Pergamos was the center for the Chaldean Mysteries, including the Priesthood and Scepter line. These same titles and credentials are now in the Papal System. You can use the Internet to verify this information, just search for the key words being highlighted. The history discovered is this:

The kings of Pergamos were both Kings and High Priests within the Chaldean Mysteries. They worshipped "**Aesculapius**", under the form of "**The Serpent**", celebrated with frantic orgies and excesses, (REF_B: Page 218). The last king, Attalus III, at his death **left by will all his dominions to the**

Roman people in BC 133", (REF_B: Page 218). One such title being transferred to Rome was "**Pontifex Maximus**".

"**Pontifex Maximus**" (Latin, literally: "greatest pontiff") was the High Priest of the "**College of Pontiffs**", **Collegium Pontificum**, in ancient Rome. This was the most important position in the ancient Roman religion, open only to patricians until BC 254. Remember, this title and "**College of Pontiffs**" existed in Rome before the Christian Era.

The "**College of Pontiffs**" (Latin Collegium Pontificum; see "**collegium**") was a body of the ancient Roman state whose members were the highest-ranking priests of the state religion. The "**Flamens**" were priests, dressed in 'red', in the "**College of Pontiffs**", in charge of fifteen official cults of Roman religion, each assigned to a particular god. The three major "**Flamens**" were the "**Flamen Dialis**", the high priest of Jupiter; the "**Flamen Martialis**", who cultivated Mars; and the "**Flamen Quirinalis**", devoted to Quirinus. The term 'Chief Priests' is translated as "**Pontifices**" in the Latin Vulgate, and 'High Priest' as "**Pontifex**" in Hebrews 2:17",
(**http://en.wikipedia.org/wiki/College_of_Pontiffs**).

The Pontifex was not simply a priest. He had both political and religious authority. Julius Caesar became Pontifex in BC 73, and "**Pontifex Maximus**" in BC 63. In AD 382, the Emperor Gratian removed the "**Altar of Victory**" from the Forum, withdrew the state subsidies that funded many pagan activities, and formally renounced the title of "**Pontifex Maximus**", (**http://en.wikipedia.org/wiki/Pontifex_Maximus**).

The Papal System's Pope took this title's authority, but has not overtly listed this title as a credential. That is, ask who is the "**Pontifex Maximus**" today, and they will answer, it is the Pope. Yet, this title is not listed among the Pope's official credentials. This of course is just a formality.

The Chaldean Mysteries has Bacchus as the High Priest passing priestly credentials down to others. Another name for Bacchus is "**Dagon, the Fish god**", and the Assyrian Dagon, wearing a "**Fish-Head Mitre**", (REF_B: Page 191). Many will notice that the Papal System's Pope, Cardinals, and Bishops wear a similar "hat", resembling a fish and open mouth.

The Papal Mitre and the “**Fish-Head Mitre**” of Dagon, both the same.

The title "**Pontifex Maximus**” is effectively claimed by the Pope of Rome, as this authority is represented by the three crowns on the “**Pope’s Tiara**” (crowning head dress).

> The first circlet, or crown, symbolizes the Pope’s “**Universal Episcopate**”. This means that he claims to be ruler over all the church of Christ. All priestly power, including the power to forgive sins, must come through him and his agents. That is, no salvation outside of the approval of the Papal System.
>
> The second crown symbolizes the “**Primacy of Jurisdiction**”, the “rulership over the whole church”. That is, all Diocese around the world, especially Rome, Constantinople, Jerusalem, Antioch, and Alexandria.
>
> The third crown symbolizes the “**Temporal Power**”, all kings, presidents, and governments are subservient to the Pope.

The “**Pope’s Tiara**” having the “**Three Crowns”** of authority.

Understood by only a very few is that the “**Pope’s Tiara**” proclaims the exact same three great authorities (crowns) as does Cush.

All hail Thee, Thoth Hermes, **Thrice Greatest** . . . Hermes, the greatest
of all "**Philosophers**", and
of all "**Priests**", and
of all "**Kings**".
These praises are the same three crowns as on the "**Pope's Tiara**":
the "**Universal Episcopate**", and
the "**Primacy of Jurisdiction**", and
the "**Temporal Power**".

Thus, what used to be the "**College of Pontiffs**" in the Chaldean Mysteries is now the "**College of Cardinals**", whose priests are still dressed in 'red', in the Papal System. What used to be the "**Pontifex Maximus**" in Pergamos is now the "**Pontifex Maximus**" in the Papal System. What used to be direct worship of the "**Triune God**" of the Chaldean and Egyptian Mysteries is now indirect worship through the renaming of the same players, using "Christian" sounding names. The same original festivals and stories are renamed and retold to sound "Christian".

The Pope also has the title of the "**High Priest of Janus**" (sometimes called '**Jove'**). The god "**Janus**" is a Roman-invention, not having a counter part in the Greek Mysteries. The two faced god "**Janus**" is Cush and Bacchus, two gods as being one god, (**http://en.wikipedia.org/wiki/Janus**).

Another primary connection is that of symbols. The primary symbols used by the Papacy are "**The Cross**" and the making of the "**Sign of the Cross**" over the chest.

The Sign of The Cross

"**The Cross**" is a well known and immediately recognized Papal symbol. But with only a quick investigation it is manifest that "**The Cross**" was a religious symbol centuries previous to Christianity. Nearly all world religions have used and still use "**The Cross**" as their own primary religious symbol, (REF_B: Page 197-205). Movie documentaries show how the "**Sign of the Cross**" is used by the Hindu priests. They too use their hands, dipped in ashes, to mark this sign on the foreheads of worshippers in ceremonies.

"That mystic '**Tau**' was **marked in baptism on the foreheads** [on the **third eye**] of those initiated in the Mysteries [all of them, Hinduism, Buddhism, Aztec], and was used in every variety of way as a most

> sacred symbol ... There is hardly a Pagan tribe where the cross has not been found", (REF_B: Page 178-179).

The "**Cross**" symbol is depicted in the letter '**T**', or "**Tau**", but is also depicted in many other similar forms. The "**Ankh**" and "**Swastika**" are also well known types of crosses, and are used in Hinduism, Buddhism, and the Egyptian Mysteries too.

In the Egyptian Mysteries this is also the symbol for "**The Apis**", which is the symbol for the Sun in the constellation of Taurus at the spring equinox. This astronomy was true circa BC 2600. "**The Crux Ansata**" is the "**Tau Cross**" with an oval above it, and is the symbol for "**Immortality**", that is, the "**Immortal Soul**" of man, (REF_C: Page 96-102).

The Egyptian Mystery's **Ankh**, symbol for Eternal Life.

William H. Prescott, in "The Conquest of Mexico", describes the astonishment of the Spanish Catholic priests when they encountered "**The Cross**" as a symbol of worship among the Aztec Indians.

> "Yet we should have charity for the missionaries who first landed in this world of wonders; where . . . they were astonished by occasional glimpses of rites and ceremonies. . . In their amazement . . . They did not inquire, whether the SAME THINGS WERE NOT PRACTICED BY OTHER IDOLATROUS PEOPLE. They could not suppress their wonder, as they behold "**The Cross**", the sacred emblem of their own faith, raised as an OBJECT OF WORSHIP in the temple of Anahuac. They met with it in various places; and the IMAGE OF A CROSS may be seen at this day, sculpted in bas-relief, on the walls of one of the buildings of Palenque, while a figure bearing some resemblance to that of a child is held up to it, as if in adoration" (p.695).

In Palenque, Mexico, founded by Votan circa BC 850, there is a temple known as the "**Temple of the Cross**." Inscribed on an altar there is a cross, 6.5 by 11.0 feet in size. These Indians had no contact with the Spanish until circa AD 1550, about 2,400 years later. It is manifest that "**The Cross**" is not a "Christian-only" symbol.

The Woman Holding a Cup

Please investigate the slogan "**Sedet super universum**", "**The whole world is her Seat**". Reading up on this reveals who "**The Woman**" is, and the direct connection to the Mysteries.

Papal Coin minted 1958. "**The Woman**" holding a Cross Staff and Cup. The Cup has in it the Sun, having **<u>Seven Spokes</u>**.

Coin showing "**The Woman**" holding a "**Cross Tipped Staff**" and Cup. Minted 1825 by Pope Leo XII. Notice the **<u>Seven Spokes</u>** around her head.

Greek Mysteries Hera (Gaia) as "**The Woman Holding the Cup**". Notice the "**Winged Tipped Staff**" was replaced by a "**Cross Tipped Staff**".

Thus, it is evident that the Papal System is the transferred Chaldean Mysteries from Pergamos, the "**Throne of Satan**", to the Pope of Rome and his agents. The Papal System is the same Chaldean and Egyptian Mysteries, symbols and rituals, but appears Christianized by using different names.

To read more about how the Papal System has Christianized the Egyptian Mysteries as well, refer to:

(**S**: "**Egyptian Book of the Dead and the Mysteries of Amenta**") and (**http://egyptianchristianity.com/egyptian_parallels_christ_jesus.htm**).

For the purposes of this presentation, <u>**the Papal System includes the Greek Orthodox Church and Protestant Organizations**</u>. The Greek Orthodox did not split until circa AD 1053, and essentially has the same structure, symbols, icons, and shrines, (**http://en.wikipedia.org/wiki/East-West_Schism**).

The Protestant splits also retained the same structure, symbols, and icons, but changed some of the names. For example priests are called pastors. Also retained are the Cross, the Crucifix, and the Trinity. The Protestant Organizations retain the same Sunday worship system, most of the same festivals, especially Christmas and Easter, and a similar hierarchal structure of pastors and bishops.

From the point of view of which "**Specific Laws**" are being practiced, the Greek Orthodox Church and Protestant Organizations follow those of the Great Dragon, and dismiss those of the YHWH.

The Genius of Using Christianized Names

<u>The genius of transforming the Chaldean and Egyptian Mysteries into Christianized names and festivals **cannot be overstated**</u>. In this Papal System people are told that they are following the God of Abraham, the YHWH, but doing so with the same worship festivals of the Chaldean and Egyptian Mysteries, and while obeying the same "**Specific Laws**" of the Great Dragon.

Essentially, this Priesthood tells people that the YHWH has changed His mind. He now says to "**worship Me this other way**", when in fact the YHWH has never said this. <u>**The people do not know any better; as they just believe and do whatever their leaders tell them**</u>.

Consider again the "**Golden Calf**" scene in Exodus 32:4-5: (quoting word-for-word) "and he made a calf casted, and they said '**these are your gods**' Israel ... and saw Aaron and he built an alter before it, and called Aaron and said '**a Feast to YHWH**' tomorrow is". This "**Golden Calf**" was the Egyptian Mysteries "Apis", which is Osiris which is Nimrod.

> "The ordinary way in which the favorite Egyptian divinity Osiris was mystically represented was under the form of a young bull or calf, the calf '**Apis**', from which the golden calf of the Israelites was borrowed", (REF_B: Page 46).

What this demonstrates is that **you cannot just change the names of the Mystery's gods**, now calling them something that sounds like they represent the YHWH, and somehow doing these name-changes fool the YHWH. You can say something is '**dedicated to YHWH**', but in fact it is not. **Christianizing the names and festivals does not change what they really are**. The YHWH is not fooled by this.

An example: you tell your kids to wash the car, using water from your house's hose, and sponges from your kitchen. They go outside to wash the car using their Dad's hose and sponges. But your neighbor comes over and **tells them that you changed your mind**. He tells them that you now say to use the water from your neighbor's hose, and to use his sponges. From the point of view of your kids, they are obeying your orders. The kids can call it "our Dad's hose" and "our Dad's sponges", but actually they are not. In reality, your neighbor **has got your kids to obey him**, and to use his things instead.

The greatest deception is to tell people that the YHWH has changed His mind, but in fact the YHWH never has. Tell people that the YHWH has changed His mind so that you now "do things" differently. Tell them that the different things are the new way of the YHWH, when in fact the new way is the way of the Great Dragon. Do this and **the people think they are worshipping the YHWH, when in fact they are not**.

Definitions of words start with the Hebrew/Aramaic Text of the YHWH, and not what the neighbors say. **It is so easy to be fooled**.

Thus, the "**Papal System**" is just another "**School of Thought**", just another Head of the Beast, worshipping the Great Dragon through his Papal Priesthood, sister organizations, and agents.

Tuesday: Mars, Bacchus

The planet Mars has both Bacchus and Ishtar as its representatives. That is, both Bacchus and Ishtar have Mars as one of their primary symbols. Both are the "**god of War and Fortresses**". From the female side point of view, this is the day for Ishtar's son and husband **Bacchus/Nimrod**.

This Head of the Seven Headed Beast **is the selfish, aggressive, and oppressive side of the Military, Nobility, and Caste System**.

The concept of war does not seem like a religious subject, but actually it is. It includes the concepts of fortresses, which are gated towns, and therefore social order. The social order includes having rank and privilege based upon who you are.

To fight a war you must have a hierarchy of command, from privates to generals. The only real physical difference between an officer in the military and a priest is the uniform. Otherwise, they both have training, appointments, rank, privileges, and tell people what to do. The substantial difference is that the priests tend to deal with the conceptual matters of life, and the officers tend to deal with the physical matters of life.

Looking at the military, you encounter an immediate caste-system. For example, the officers have their own Lounge, where the privates cannot go. What is being described is a "**School of Thought**" in which you have rank and privilege based upon who you are. Just as with priests, officers are groomed and appointed for advancement, which makes them "somebody of consequence".

Like a religion, the military and social order behind the fortified walls is a community ruled by a "**School of Thought**", a way of thinking, which is thereby a religious system. Just as in the Chaldean Mysteries it is taught that there are good guys and bad guys. Your officers follow the "**Good Side of the Force**", and the enemy's officers follow the "**Dark Side of the Force**". An army can go to war to defend your hearth and home, or it can go to war to attack another's hearth and home. An army can protect the good people of the land, or it can be their biggest bully.

Having social status, rank in terms of responsibilities, and showing respect to those working honestly and hard, is not worshipping the Great Dragon. What is worshipping the Great Dragon is combining this "**School of Thought**" with selfishness, greed, envy, oppression, and meanness.

For example, a Captain in the army has a certain social standing in his community, and may be asked to set at the front of the dinner table. This is not the "**School of Thought**" being depicted by the symbol of Mars. The switch is when the Captain's mindset turns aggressive, and then bullies and hurts others for his own gain.

There is a difference in "**School of Thought**" between a ruler who has an army to work rivers and bridges, versus a ruler who has an army raping and pillaging the communities of others.

The world we see, the pervasive "**School of Thought**" of history, is that the "**god of War**" is the mindset excusing one army to attack another. We see similar deeds done in social circles, allowing snobbery, scornful conduct, selfish politics, and deceitful slandering of others.

It is through this twisted "**School of Thought**" that the Great Dragon fulfills one of his primary goals. Ultimately, **his goal is the unfulfilled potential and the literal oblivion** of those created in the image of the YHWH. Throughout the course of history, how many billions of people were victimized by this "**School of Thought**"? How many were killed before their time? Do you want to count the unborn too? How many never reached their full potential because they were oppressed, maimed, malnourished, denied education, robbed, or enslaved? Is it a stretch to suggest that 90% of all those ever born have fallen victim to this twisted "**School of Thought**" of the "**god of War and Fortresses**"?

Thus, the selfish, aggressive, and oppressive side of the "**Military, Nobility, and Caste System**" is just another "**School of Thought**", just another Head of the Beast, worshipping the Great Dragon through his "**Military and Social Elite**" Priesthood and agents.

Wednesday: Mercury, Cush

The planet Mercury has both Cush and Ishtar as its representatives. That is, both Cush and Ishtar have Mercury as one of their primary symbols. Both are the "**gods of Medicine**". From the female side point of view, this is the day for Ishtar's brother and first husband **Cush**, or Thoth.

This Head of the Seven Headed Beast **is the Medicine and Healing Enlightenment, the Shaman System**.

Most are familiar with the term "**Faith Healer**". This is someone who heals a physical ailment of another by words and rituals to muster the unseen powers of some external force. Some Christians engage in "**Faith Healing**", wherein the words used might be a prayer, or a series of commanding shouts to invoke the powers of the "**Holy Ghost**". The ritual might be loud music with drums, hand gestures, dances, and rhythmic voice intensities.

What may be unpopular is to point out that this style of "**Faith Healing**" is also performed by Shamans, Witch Doctors, Medicine Men, and Psychics. The words used might also be a prayer to a deity, or a series of commanding shouts for powers to manifest. The ritual also might be loud music with drums, hand gestures, dances, and rhythmic voice intensities. The reader might be able to understand this connection better by remembering movies where they have seen westerns, wherein Indian "**Medicine Men**" do their chanting dance magic around a campfire.

The obvious question becomes, to which deity or external force is the "**Faith Healer**" asking for manifestation? As discussed earlier, you probably should not say "Amen" to a "**Faith Healer's**" prayer, unless you know three things. Remember, **just because they say the right words, does not mean they are directing those words to the right supernatural Being**. Just because they say the right words **does not mean that they have the right definitions of those words**. They might be saying something entirely different than what you think they are saying. And thirdly, just because they are "**a good person**" **does not mean they are praying to the right supernatural Being either**.

<u>**It is in the best interest of the Great Dragon to answer prayers and to perform miracles**</u> in order to increase the credibility of his agents. It is not a matter of being "black and white". It is a matter of being sure you know to which supernatural Being or agents are being sought out for their healing-powers. **Many "Faith Healers" do indeed get startling results**. People are healed, magic does happen, and miracles are witnessed. If they had a 100% failure rate, no one would ever ask them to do anything again.

Even the Messiah tells us that "**Faith Healers**" do perform miracles:

> "<u>Not every one</u> that saith unto me, Lord, Lord, shall enter into the kingdom of heaven; <u>but he that doeth the will of my Father</u> which is in heaven. <u>Many will say to me in that day</u>, Lord, Lord, have we not prophesied in thy name? And <u>in thy name have cast out devils</u>? <u>And in thy name done many wonderful works</u>? And then will I profess unto them, <u>**I never knew you**</u>: **depart from me**, ye that work [Greek is 'anti-law'] iniquity" (**Matthew 7:21-23**).

The criteria for judging "**Faith Healers**" is not that they get results. The criteria for judging "**Faith Healers**" is that <u>**they teach and practice the teachings of the YHWH**</u>.

The success of a "**Faith Healer**" to "do things" is not the criteria. What must be determined is the source of the power being sought out by the "**Faith Healer**". The problem is that "**Faith Healers**" do not just "do things" physically. Far too often they also become people's spiritual counselor and teacher too. **It is easy to be fooled**.

Always refer to Deuteronomy chapter 13: even if it comes to pass, if they do not tell you to only obey the YHWH's teachings, then do not believe them, and cast them aside.

Many will notice that the often used symbol for the medical profession is the "**Winged Rod, Entwined with Serpents**". This is the very same rod, staff, held by Cush and Gaia. The Mysteries teach that Cush, as Thoth, provided the wisdom and enlightenment in the art of medicine and healing.

"**Winged Rod, Entwined with Serpents**". The "**Rod of Asclepius**", remains the symbol of Medicine today.

There is no doubt of a connection by symbol. The connection is the science or art of using medicines, pharmaceuticals, in the process of healing people. "**Faith Healers**" often use "concoctions" as medicines, and modern doctors do the same thing with prescription drugs. But remember that the New Testament author Luke was a Physician, and no doubt also used "concoctions" of herbs and tinctures as medicines. It is manifest that Luke talked to and obeyed the YHWH through the Messiah. Thus, the connection is not that someone is acting as a Physician and engaged in trying to heal using "concoctions". The connection is made when the Physician **starts to seek a higher power during the process**. To which higher power is the Physician talking to, as he seeks that higher power to diagnose and heal? It is easy to be fooled.

Most would argue that our modern medical Doctors typically do not seek a higher power as they do their diagnosis and prescription drugs processes to heal. The issue then is: "What if they do?" Do you say "Amen"?

Thus, the "**Shaman System**" is just another "**School of Thought**", just another Head of the Beast, worshipping the Great Dragon through his "**Shaman**" Priesthood and agents.

Saturday: Saturn, Osiris

Explaining the left side leg of the weekday pyramid starts with Saturday. Again, each of the planets has both a male side and a female side, both a male and female god representation. The planet Saturn has both Cush and Rhea/Isis as its representatives. That is, both Cush and Isis have Saturn as one of their primary symbols. Osiris also has Saturn as his symbol, because he received it from his father Cush.

The left side of the weekday pyramid, Saturday, Friday, Thursday, have their focus on **Osiris**. That is, from the male point of view, how do "things" relate to Osiris? Saturday represents Osiris himself, the son, brother, and husband of Isis. In this male side of the Mysteries, the men (Priests) can have sex with women; and the women (Priestesses) can have sex with men.

This Head of the Seven Headed Beast **is the Freemason System**, which typically depict the stories and symbols of the Egyptian Mysteries. The Freemason System has also incorporated several key aspects of the Caldean Mysteries as well.

In the Freemason System, the primary fraternities are "**Men Only**", with other fraternities as "**Women Only**". The history of the Freemason System goes back to circa BC 2600, as evidenced by its own astronomical symbols, (REF_A: Page 16, 107, REF_C).

In the Egyptian Mysteries Osiris is the dominant male god. Osiris is the "**Man with the Bull's Head**" and the "**Father of the gods**", and the "**god of the Afterlife**". He is depicted as a man sitting on his heavenly throne as the Judge of all men's souls in the afterlife. The Triune God is Osiris, Isis, and Horus, with 'Hiram' sometimes used as an alternative name for Horus. The Triune God is also "Isis, Horus, Seb", that is, "**The Mother**, the Incarnate god **Child**, and the **Father of the gods**", (REF_B: Page 153).

Many are familiar with the degrees or levels of an American Freemason fraternity. At the core what they teach is this:

> "...Freemasonry, teaching the two great doctrines of **the unity of God, as One Eternal Spiritual Being**, and **the immortality of the soul of man**..." (REF_A: Page 108).
>
> "At our assemblies meet in harmony the Christian, the Hebrew, the Mohammedan, the Buddhist, and the Brahman, the followers of Confucius and the disciples of Zoroaster. At the masonic altar all these may offer their adoration to the same **great Architect of the universe** -- thus presenting a sublime spectacle of the 'fatherhood of God and the brotherhood of man'." (REF_A: Page 111)

Notice the use of the same titles as the Great Dragon, and the importance of the "**immortality of the soul**". With only a quick investigation it is verified that the symbols and rituals used in Freemasonry parallel and mimic the Egyptian Mysteries, focused on Osiris.

The worship of Moloch and the planet Saturn was a proclivity of Israel throughout the Hebrew/Aramaic Text. This worship of another god is cited in Acts 7:43; (quoting word-for-word) "And you took up **the tabernacle the of Moloch** [G3434/H4432] and the **star of the god of you Rephan** [G4481] the images that you made to worship them and I will remove you beyond Babylon." The star Remphan is the planet Saturn, (**http://en.wikipedia.org/wiki/Remphan**). Moloch (Jeremiah 32:35) is the Chaldean Bel is Nimrod is the Egyptian Osiris, (REF_B: Page 118). Thus, the false worship system of Baal is the worshipping of Nimrod/Osiris, symbolized by the planet Saturn. The tabernacle, tent, of Moloch represents the Priesthood of the Great Dragon found in the Mysteries founded by Osiris and Isis.

Thus, the "**Freemason System**" is just another "**School of Thought**", just another Head of the Beast, worshipping the Great Dragon through his "**Osiris**" Priesthood and agents.

Friday: Venus, Isis

The planet Venus has both Osiris and Isis as its representatives. That is, both Osiris, as Vulcan, and Isis have Venus as one of their primary symbols.

Friday represents **Isis** with Wisdom and Love, with the mindset of looking at Cush and/or Osiris as her husbands, and herself as "**The Adored**" and "**The Mother**". In this female side of the Mysteries, "**Spiritual Enlightenment**" and energies are seen as coming from the female qualities of the human soul.

This Head of the Seven Headed Beast **is the Hinduism / Oriental (Chi) System**, which typically depict things using the symbols of the Egyptian Mysteries, but with Oriental/Sanskrit names. In this System Cush is the "**Supreme Being**", and Osiris is one of the primary god-players.

From (**http://en.wikipedia.org/wiki/Hinduism**):
Categorized as an "Eastern Religion", Hinduism has many branches, including Oriental branches, and is described as both a religion and a way of living, as a traditional way of life. Many practitioners refer to Hinduism as "**Sanatana Dharma**", the "**Eternal Law**" or the "**Eternal Way**". This title "**The Way**" is what Thoth did after talking to the Great Dragon.

> "But others, casting themselves before the feet of Hermes [Thoth], besought him to teach them the **Way of Life**", (REF_C).

Hinduism teaches:

> "Brahman, the supreme soul ['**Supreme Being**'] that is present in everything and everyone", and "Most Hindus believe that the spirit or **soul** – the true 'self' of every person, called the atman - **is eternal**".

Many in the Oriental branches cater to their dead ancestors, thinking they are still alive in the afterlife, as a dominate portion of their lifestyle. Hinduism also worships the angelic agents of the Great Dragon also:

> "The Hindu scriptures refer to celestial entities called **Devas** ..., '**the shining ones**', which may be translated into English as 'gods' or '**heavenly beings**' ",

Hindu Statue of the god **Shiva** (Horus)
Notice the "**Trident Staff**", the "**All Seeing Eye**",
and "**Serpents**" around the neck and arms.

Thus, the "**Hinduism System**" is just another "**School of Thought**", just another Head of the Beast, worshipping the Great Dragon through his "**Hinduism**" Priesthood and agents.

Thursday: Jupiter, the Great Dragon

The planet Jupiter is by far the most confusing. Jupiter has several males, Cush, Bacchus, and Ninus (Horus) and two females, Gaia and Ishtar as its representatives. That is, all of these gods have Jupiter as one of their primary symbols. This of course leads to much confusion about whom or what Jupiter represents in any statue or storyline. Sometimes a story uses the name "Jupiter-puer", which always refers to Horus as a child. Otherwise, it is an educated guess based on other clues that may or may not be present.

Thursday represents **Cush** with ultimate Wisdom and "**Spiritual Enlightenment**", with the mindset of looking at "life" as the endless search for the "**Superior Way**". That is, a god is not worshipped; rather the concept of "**Spiritual Enlightenment**" is worshipped. In this male side of the Mysteries, "**Spiritual Enlightenment**" and its energies are depicted as coming from the male qualities of the human intellect.

This Head of the Seven Headed Beast **is the Buddhist and Humanistic System**, which typically depict things using the symbols of the Chaldean Mysteries, but often with Oriental/Sanskrit names. In this System the "**Supreme Being**" is **the Great Dragon when he is not manifested in any visible form**. It is the Great Dragon as "**The Supreme Mind**" of everything, eternal, and always present in everything.

The following is taken from (**http://en.wikipedia.org/wiki/Buddhism**):
Also categorized as an "Eastern Religion", Buddhism has many branches, including Oriental branches, and is also described as both a religion and a way of living, as a traditional way of life.

In Buddhism there is no "**Creator God**", not the way most people would mean it.

> "Since the time of the Buddha, the refutation [rejection] of the existence of a Creator Deity has been seen as a key point in distinguishing Buddhist from non-Buddhist views... Buddhism **rejects the concepts** of a permanent self or an unchanging, **eternal soul**, as it is called in Hinduism and Christianity... **Karma** (from

> Sanskrit: "action, work") **is the force** that drives **Samsara** - the [endless] cycle of suffering and rebirth for each being... Buddhism does not involve belief in a **creator God** who has control over human destiny... [some branches] who stressed that the soul must be freed from matter... Each rebirth takes place within one of five realms according to Theravadins... the idea that the Buddha taught of an intermediate stage between one life and the next".

In Buddhism there is the mindset that there is no supernatural Being responsible for creation and souls living on in an afterlife. From this "**School of Thought**" comes "**Humanism**", reinforced by the scientific illusion of "**Evolution**" and "**Darwinism**" taking the place of "God".

However, the presentation of **the Buddhism "School of Thought" is just "word-play"; it is an "intellectual game"**. For examples, instead of saying there is a "**Creator God**"; Buddhism redefines him into two separate things. That is, "God" is now "**the supernatural force**" that drives everything, and is the "**Samsara**", a magically existing process ("**The Supreme Mind**" of everything) where after death a person, [being very careful not to call it a "soul"], is eventually given another body, and is reincarnated to live again, always repeating in an endless cycle. This "**Samsara**" of course is the same thing as "**The Lie**". It is still an immortal soul, just with the afterlife's states and gates being presented differently.

Even understanding the above, Buddhism also teaches that there are supernatural Beings.

> The Buddha said that **devas** (translated as 'gods') **do exist**, but they were regarded as still being trapped in **Samsara** [the endless cycle of suffering and rebirth], and are **not necessarily wiser than us**. In fact, **the Buddha is often portrayed as a teacher of the gods, and superior to them**.

Adding even more confusion is that some branches of Buddhism also teach a "**Trinity**".

> "In Japan, the Buddhists worship their great divinity, Buddha, with three heads, in the very same form, under the name of '**San Pao Fuh**'. All these have existed from ancient times. While overlaid with idolatry, the recognition of a **Trinity** was universal in all the ancient nations of the world, proving how deep-rooted in the human race was the primeval doctrine on this subject, which comes out so distinctly in Genesis", (REF_B: Page 18).

Other branches teach that the Buddha has three kayas or bodies:

1. The Dharmakaya or Truth body which embodies the very principle of enlightenment and knows no limits or boundaries;
2. The Sambhogakaya or body of mutual enjoyment which is a body of bliss or **clear light manifestation**;
3. The Nirmanakaya or created **body which manifests in time and space**.

(**http://en.wikipedia.org/wiki/Trikaya**).

Essentially, this teaches that "You do not have a Soul, You are a Soul, and You have a Body". Looking closer at these three bodies of Buddha it is noticed that:

1. The Truth body is the "**Spiritual Enlightenment**" coming directly from the Great Dragon, just as Cush received;
2. The body of **clear light** is the immortal soul, existing even after death without a physical body;
3. The **body which manifests in time and space** is the promised new body obtained in the afterlife, and reincarnated into a physical body again.

Thus, the "**Buddhism System**" is just another "**School of Thought**", just another Head of the Beast, worshipping the Great Dragon through his "**Buddhist**" Priesthood and agents.

The Islamic Religion

It is reasonable to ask about the Islamic Religion, wondering to which of the above seven "**Schools of Thought**" of the Great Dragon it may follow. This question is reasonable, but the answer is not so straight forward.

Islam is a monotheistic religion which is practiced by around 19% of the world population. It is important to note that the Islamic Religion itself cannot be one of the seven "**Schools of Thought**", since it only began very recently in history, circa AD 610.

Perhaps unpopular to say in our modern western culture, but the Koran, and the core concepts at the foundation of the Islamic Religion, do not appear to directly follow any of the seven "**Schools of Thought**" of the Great Dragon. For example, it is an absolute tenet of Islam to utterly reject the worshipping of a "**Triune God**", and to worship the God of Abraham as "**The Only God**". This includes refraining from bowing down to idols, and not practicing the festivals of the gods found in the Mysteries.

There is also some ambiguity as to how Islam teaches "**The Lie**" regarding the immortality of the soul. In Islam there are "**Muslim Philosophers**". Historically, these are men who spent a great deal of their lives interpreting the Koran. Similar to the Jewish Religion having "**Rabbis**" and "**The Talmud**", different "**Muslim Philosophers**" have taught differing ideas about a man's "**rational soul**" after death. Most of the different interpretations stem from having differences in the definitions of some key Arabic words, especially the definition of "the soul".

Generally, the Koran has the "**rational souls**" of the dead kept in a place called the "**Barzakh**". However, the Koran also has text allowing the "**Muslim Philosophers**" to further speculate as to what the souls are doing while they are awaiting the great Judgment event (the resurrection).

Some interpretations have the "**rational souls**" fully alive, conversing with other "**rational souls**", even reuniting with their own dead bodies on occasion. Some "**Muslim Philosophers**" have the "**rational souls**" receiving both punishments (for evil deeds) and rewards (the 70 virgins), which of course requires the "**rational souls**" to be alive. Others have the "**rational souls**" mostly waiting around for the Judgment.
(**www.islamicinformation.net/2008/05/souls-journey-after-death-in-islam.html**).
Such interpretations of the Koran have the Islamic religion teaching some version of "**The Lie**" of the Great Dragon.

There are also many important differences between the worship practices of the Islamic Religion and the Specific Laws of the YHWH. For examples: the Friday Sabbath versus the Saturday Sabbath; and the Holy Days of Islam versus the Holy Days of the YHWH.

We observe that the Koran teaches about Yahoshua (Jesus) as being a prophet, but it does not acknowledge Yahoshua as being the resurrected and exalted Messiah of the whole world.

Such differences become more clearly understood when said this way:

> "The Islamic Religion does not worship the Elohim/God of Abraham, and Isaac, and Israel (Jacob)."
>
> "The Islamic Religion does worship the Elohim/God of Abraham and Ishmael".

Viewed from this perspective it is predictable that there will be significant differences in how the Elohim/God of Abraham is worshipped. Following the

"**Melchizedek Priesthood**" prophet Abraham, through Abraham's son Ishmael, does not automatically mean that they are worshipping the Great Dragon.

From a point of view, **the Islamic Religion may be a branch of the "Melchizedek Priesthood" of the YHWH through Abraham**, just as other branches have existed through history. But to be fair, it is also possible that the Islamic Religion is not a **"Melchizedek Priesthood"** branch, but is just another organization of men.

Regardless, the Islamic Religion does not follow the "**Melchizedek Priesthood**" prophet Abraham, through the Priesthood line of Abraham, Isaac, and Jacob (Israel), **on to Yahoshua, the current High Priest and the Messiah of the YHWH**.

Thus, we observe that the Islamic Religion appears to have a confused mixture of teachings, some taken from the Great Dragon and some taken from the YHWH. For these reasons, this presentation is not going to list the Islamic Religion under any of the seven "**Schools of Thought**"; purposefully "keeping this open" for further discussion.

SUMMARY

The goal of this presentation is to provide enough of an understanding of the names, titles, and symbols used in the Mysteries, to be forewarned.

Many readers may feel overwhelmed upon realizing the full ramifications of all of this information. It is hoped that you will now understand that the whole world is worshipping the Great Dragon through his System, The Beast with Seven Heads. The Priesthood and agents of the Great Dragon are everywhere, from schools to religions to politics. His Seven "**Schools of Thought**" are infused into every aspect of culture, and his "**Specific Laws**" are automatically accepted as "**God's Own Truth**" by nearly everyone you meet and encounter on mass media.

The Hebrew Text makes it clear that the YHWH looks at a person's heart, their kidneys, to make judgments about the quality of their devotion to Him. This author is not going to be presumptuous enough to guess how the YHWH judges individual people; as He views each one of them as individuals, as a person who is entrapped and exploited by whatever confused mixture of the "Schools of Thought" the Great Dragon has them.

But the problem is, since the worship of the Great Dragon is so much a part of the culture and mindset of the whole world, how do the worshippers of the YHWH get out of her, as told in Revelation 18:1-5?

Consider: that it is very easy for "them" to spot you, as all you have to do is to keep a lifestyle obeying the "**Specific Laws**" of the YHWH. Is your coming out of Babylon, and not worshipping the Beast, mean you need to go someplace where you cannot be spotted?

It is sobering to remember that "**Religious Freedom**" is a recent luxury. Historically, most worshippers of the YHWH had no such "right" or "privilege", and found themselves directly persecuted by their own neighbors, churches, and governments. It is not any stretch to suggest that this same historical reality is soon to reappear.

With the information given herein, it is apparent that most of the names, titles, and symbols we see around us do mean to tell us something. Too often the symbols seen on church buildings, and the titles sung in songs, include the same as those reserved to signal the worship of the Great Dragon, his Priesthood, and his agents. If you can see these, **then you are forewarned** that something is just not right.

By having an understanding of the names, titles, and symbols used in the Mysteries to represent the worship of the Great Dragon, his Priesthood, and his agents, you are forewarned that many things around you are not right. Understanding that you should not believe "**The Lie**", and understanding why you keep the "**Specific Laws**" of the YHWH, will give you an insight needed to resist the Adversary, and to not be overwhelmed by him, or his agents, or your friends.

The YHWH, and His resurrected and exalted Messiah Yahoshua, want everyone to wake up and see what is going on. Remember the words of the Messiah Yahoshua in Mark 12:29-30:

> "<u>The first of all the commandments is</u>, Hear, O Israel; **The Lord our God is one ['1'] Lord**: And thou **shalt love** the Lord thy God with **all thy heart**, and with **all thy soul**, and with **all thy mind**, and with **all thy strength**: this is the first commandment."

Seek the YHWH **with your whole heart**, and obey His "**Specific Laws**", **<u>because you want to</u>**.

APPENDIX A: Details of The Priesthood of Cush

Surviving the flood was Noah, his three sons, and their wives, (Genesis 9:18). Noah's three sons were Shem, Ham, and Japheth, each son was essentially the King of their own family clan. Each family clan was supposed to migrate in different directions to re-populate the earth.

For this presentation, the important family genealogy to follow is that of Ham. Ham's genealogy is both important and complicated, so it will be shown using the table below.

The Line from Ham To Horus

Ham (Bible name) The "**god of Heaven/Air**" The male DNA of Noah	**Gaia** (Greek) The Female DNA of Cain	
		Cush (Bible name) Son of Ham & Gaia Now the Male DNA of Cain. The "**god of Earth**"
		Astarte (Chaldean) Rhea (Roman) Daughter of Ham & Gaia Sister of Cush. Female DNA of Cain

Cush as Ra (Egyptian) Cush as Zeus (Greek) Takes titles and wives of Ham, including his mother Gaia (by force). Now Cush has the title of being the "god of both Heaven and Earth"	**Astarte** becomes sister & wife of Cush	
	(the very same) **Astarte** Gives birth to Nimrod, thus is the sister & mother of Osiris	**Nimrod** (Bible) Osiris (Egyptian) Son of Cush & Astarte Brother of Astarte The "**god of the Sea / Underworld**" (Abyss)

Nimrod (Bible) Osiris (Egyptian) Is given titles and wives of Cush, including his mother Astarte. Now Osiris has triple title: the god of Heaven and Earth and Sea	(the very same) **Astarte** Now Isis, as the mother & sister & wife of Osiris	
Osiris is executed by Set (Shem) for rebellion		
	Isis (Egyptian) (the very same) **Astarte** as the "Virgin Mother" gives birth to Horus	**Horus** (Egyptian) Son of Cush-Osiris & Isis Born from a "Miracle Birth" is the "Only Begotten" Incarnated "Son of god" Legally is the son of Osiris, but DNA is the son of Cush
	(the very same) **Astarte** **Nephthys** (Egyptian) As the nursing "Mother of god" (Horus)	

The Priesthood of Cain was continued after the Flood through Cush. Ham could not be a High Priest of the line of Cain, because he was a DNA son of Noah, and had no DNA of Cain. Ham's son Cush was the first male born (Genesis 10:6) to survive his father Ham eating his own children. Having the DNA of Cain, Cush became the "**Father of the gods**".

There are only five people who are the primary "gods": Gaia, Cush, Astarte, Nimrod, and Horus. There are lists of the "primary gods" having more than five names, but these lists include the same person using different names. One of the Egyptian lists has nine names, and includes Ham too, since Egypt is the "land of Ham" (Mizraim).

These "gods" were real people, which lived and died. Because of "**The Lie**" of the Great Dragon, it is taught that these people's immortal souls lived on after death, having full memory, personality, and awareness, just as they had before death. Each of these gods is seen as a different star in the night sky. For example, Osiris is the man of the constellation Orion, (REF_B: Page 15), and is the "Dog Star", Sirius, in the constellation of Canis Major. Each of these gods is associated with different planets, symbols, and character traits. (**http://en.wikipedia.org/wiki/Sirius**).

Part of the complication is that each person has multiple names, found in the differing Myths and languages. Most of the complication is because the same person has multiple names for each different thing they are doing or arena they are watching over.

For example, just consider Astarte. She has a different name as the daughter of Ham, the sister of Cush, the wife of Cush, the mother of Osiris, the wife of Osiris, the miraculously impregnated birthing mother of Horus, and the nursing mother of Horus. There are more, as she also has different names for her association with the star Sirius, the Moon, the Nile, and the canopy of the Night sky. For more on this theme see a full list of Egyptian hieroglyphs at, (**archive.org/stream/egyptianhierogly01budguoft#page/242/mode/2up**: **Page CIII-CV**).

When verifying the information contained herein, Wikipedia is a great source to start. Remember that each of these gods have different names in each language, have more than one name based on what they are doing at the time of the story or the picture drawn, and most confusing of all, they inherited the same names, titles, wives, and symbols from their fathers. That is, they became what their father was, plus what they became.

Table of the Names of the Mystery's Gods

The following table is an accumulated summary of the numerous Mysteries and Myths, such as Egyptian, Babylonian, Greek, Roman, Hindu, Buddhist, Oriental, and Freemasonry. What is presented is the composite view, keeping track of the players after putting the stories/Myths together. Shown are the various names for the five major players, "gods": Gaia, Cush, Astarte, Nimrod, and Horus. There may be mistakes in this table; this author is not going to claim infallibility in regards to tracking all of the numerous names and escapades these gods have accumulated.

Language	Gaia and Ham	Cush
Planets / Symbols	Wife of Ham, "Mother Earth", Ham is Uranus	Mercury, Saturn, "Father of the gods", "**The Eye of Ra**", a "**Serpent**", the Symbols × † ☿
Sumerian	Antu, Ham is Anu, "**god of the Air / Sky / Heaven**"	Enlil, "**god of the Earth**"
Egyptian	Nehe-māut	Tehuti / Tchehuti / Thoth, Ptah, Seb /Keb /Geb, That, Menes, Nub / Num, Khnemu / Khnum / Xnemu, Tanen
Babylonian, Asia Minor	Ninlil, Ham was Marduk	Nebo or Nabu as Mercury, Bel, Khus, Khaos, (plus the names of Ham), Asher & Anu & Hea as a " † ", Taautus
In the Gilgamesh Epic		Vater Des Jagers
Greek	Gaia / Rhea as wife of Ham, Hera as wife of Cush (Ham was Kronos, Chiron)	Hermes, Thoth, took name Kronos, Zeus, Chaos, Poseidon, Aesculapius
Roman	Terra	Mercury, Hermes, Jupiter, **Janus**
Other		Brahma, Odin, Zalmoxis

Language	Nimrod	Astarte	Horus
Planets / Symbols	Saturn, Rising Sun, Symbols "**The Bull**", "**The Horned One**"	Venus, Moon, "**Queen of Heaven**"	Jupiter, Mercury, Setting Sun, Symbols " ✝ ", Symbol "**The Circle**"
Sumerian	Ea, Ia, Enki, Abzu, "**god of the Sea / Underworld**"	Ninlil, Inanna, Innan	
Egyptian	Osirus, Shun, Athothis, Anubis, Kamut, Xennu	Isis, Nephthys, Hept, Maat, Uenephes, Henneit, Athor, Net	Horus, "**Osiris Incarnate**"
Babylonian, Asia Minor	Bacchus, Belus, Ninus, Nebu, Nin, Baal, Tammuz, Adonis, Vulcan, Marduk, Oannes, Dagon	Astarte, Ishtar, Beltis, Ashtoreth, Mylitta	Ninus (child), Ninyas, Zero, Kenkenes, Tammuz, (plus all the names of Bacchus)
In the Gilgamesh Epic	Vater Des Enmerud ?, Jager	Damuzi	Gilgamesch
Greek	Ninus, Poseidon, Adonis, Orion, Dionysus, Herakles	Cybele, Artemis, Circe, Athena, Leto, Demeter	Eros, Apollo, Iacchus, Harpocrates
Roman	Bacchus, Neptune, Dagon, Pluto, Ruder	Minerva [Etruscan], Rhea, Juno, Diana	Cupid, Apollo, Jupiter-puer
Other	Balder	Vishnu	Shiva

Some Details about the Names and Symbols

- Asher (Cush) was the supreme God of the Assyrians. **Cush even deified his own phallus**: Asher is Cush's penis, Anu is his right testis, and Hea is his left testis. These three "gods" form the Symbol " ✝ " (look at it upside down), the original "Tau" or "**Cross**". To verify this search on the term "**Herma**", and observe that the "**Herm Phallus**" looks like an inverted " ✝ ". There is no doubt that the " ✝ " is a phallic symbol, **but visualizing the penis and two testicles as three separate gods is not generally understood**. Once you see this "hidden meaning" of the " ✝ ", you will then notice that the female

"**Yoni**" (the Pudenda, the Vulva) or the "**Egg**" (as a simple circle or sphere) is often in the scene too. (**http://www.sacred-texts.com/sex/asw/index.htm**)

- "**The Circle**" representing Tammuz the resurrected Nimrod, reborn.
- Cush is Bel "**The Confounder**", as in the 'One Who Mixes It Up'. "But after that Mercury interpreted the speeches of men (whence an interpreter is called Hermeneutes), the same individual distributed the nations. Then discord began", (REF_B: Page 26).
- Cush is Mercury as Nebo or Nabu, "**Wisdom**" (itself).
- Cush's staff's head-piece is the sign of Mercury ☿ .
  Notice it has three parts:
  1.) the " † " as "**The Cross**",
  2.) the "**Yoni**", sometimes depicted as "**The Sun**" ʘ or a simple circle, "**Egg**", and
  3.) the "**Serpent**" (typically as a half-moon arc showing the heads of two serpents).
- Cush took all titles and names of Ham (Uranus), so he became the "**god of Heaven and of Earth**".
- Brahma of Hindu is Cush, who also is said to have created himself double, both male and female.
- Gaia, "**Mother Earth**", also "**Mother of the gods**". This title was also given to Isis, as Horus' descendants were gods too.
- Henneit, "**Neit is Victorious**".
- Hept, the "**Veiled One**".
- Hermes, the "**Burnt One**" (probably as the color of his skin). Also "**The Good Shepard**", carrying a lamb across shoulders.
- Ishtar, the "**Goddess of Love and War**".
- Isis as the "**Birth-Mother**", conception and incarnation of Horus.
- **Janus** (two faces as one god) as Cush and Bacchus, the primary god of the Romans. "**Janus is the gatekeeper**" in the underworld. Also, "**Janus**" as the Male and Female "**Doorkeepers**" of "**Spiritual Enlightenment**".

  (**http://en.wikipedia.org/wiki/Sol_(mythology)**)

"Janus was a dual godhead."

Two Heads: one female (no beard), the other male (with beard).
As a note: "**Ianeus**" (Ιανευσ the Gatekeeper) adds up to "**666**".

- There is also "**Janus Quadrifrons**" with four faces. He is recited first in all prayers, so that "through Me, the "**Doorkeeper**", you may attain **access to whatever Gods you please**".
- Marduk (pronounced 'Merodach') often meant simply "god".
- Menes, "**The Establisher**", as in creator.
- Nephthys is Isis as the "**Nursing-Mother**" of Horus.
- Ninus, the head of the "**Fire Worshipper**", associated with the sun.
- Oannes as the personified "**Resurrected Bacchus**" entity.
- Osiris received Cush's titles, so became the "**god of Heaven, Earth, and Sea (which is also the Underworld and the Abyss)**".
- "**Queen of Heaven**", is Astarte as the Mother and Sister and Wife of Nimrod.
- Ruder, was worshipped as one of the Roman "**Triune Gods**".
- Shun, the black son of Cush (probably the color of his skin). There are stories about Nimrod being so disfigured by fire-flames that he was considered very ugly. The contrast of these stories is that his wife Isis was considered to be the most beautiful woman in the world, married to the ugliest man in the world. "In Egypt the, fair Horus, the son of the black Osiris", (REF_B: Page 67).
- Saturn, the festival of "**Saturnalia**", now called Christmas.
- Shiva in Hindu is Horus; his symbol is also the "**Trident Staff**" symbol of authority, "**Trihsula**", and a crescent moon.
- Uenephes (Isis), the woman Pharaoh who ruled Egypt after the death of Horus. Horus died in a boar hunting accident, thus the need to sacrifice and eat swine at festivals.
- Zero, is Hebrew and Chaldean for "**The Seed**", from which comes the name "**Druid**" (namely in England), (REF_B: Page 84).

A Closer Look at The Ankh

The Egyptian Ankh is often depicted in Egyptian scenes. The Ankh symbolizes "**Eternal Life**" because it depicts **male-female procreation**. It is the **Asher-phallus** "**T**" of Cush, joined with the female "**Yoni**" of Astarte. The female "**Yoni**" can also be symbolized as a simple "**Egg**".

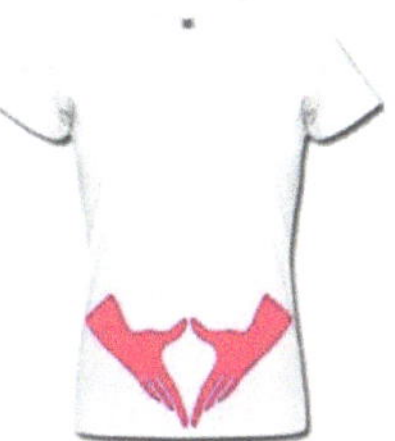

Hands making the female "**Yoni**" sign (the Pudenda or Vulva).

A "**Cross on a Calvary**".
This is the **Asher-phallus** "**T**" joined with the female "**Yoni**".

The Egyptian "**Ankh**", is also called the "**Crux Ansata**".
The female "**Yoni**" united with the male "**Phallus**".
Thus depicting procreation, and thus meaning Eternal Life.

"The Coptic Church accepted the Ankh as a Christian symbol as early as the fourth century. In a number of murals and carvings from the 4th to the 9th century, the ankh is shown together with a Greek cross and a Chi Rho", (**http://www.crosscrucifix.com/glossaryhome.htm**).

The following image shows the use of the Ankh in Hinduism. In this image notice the "**Ankh**" is used to depict the male-side joining with the female-side of Brahma. Notice that the right-hand-side is the male-side, and the left is the female-side. Also depicted are the "**All Seeing Eye**" and the "**Serpent**".

In Hinduism, Brahma created himself as a double,
as both a Male and a Female god.
(**http://en.wikipedia.org/wiki/Ardhanarishvara**)

APPENDIX B: Details of The Astrology of the Mysteries

There is a huge difference between astrology and astronomy. Astrology needs the science of astronomy to exist, but then imagines what is observed in the heavens into religious omens and powers. Astrology uses the science of astronomy, and then assigns mystical meanings to the observed heavens.

Understand: the foundation behind astrology is "**The Lie**". The "**Host of Heaven**" (the sun, moon, and planets) have a mystical and physical influence on people's lives (horoscopes) because of the belief that the gods of those planets are alive, and do things on earth. These gods can watch, listen, and influence events because, their immortal souls are taught to be still alive.

Table of Zodiac Constellations, Circa BC 2600

The following table shows the equinoxes and solstices around the year BC 2600. Included are the assignments made to the constellations by the Mysteries. There are some significant differences between this table and modern astrology. Differences are the result of the precession of the equinoxes, wherein the shifting of the equinoxes and solstices move year by year, through one constellation into another. This table shows what the astronomy was when Cush, Isis, Osiris, and Horus started the Mysteries.

Zodiac	Star	Planet	God	Four Pillars	Notes
Aries					the Ram
Taurus	Aldebaran	Sun / Mercury	**Cush** / **Thoth**	Spring, The Bull	the Bull, (**Earth**)
Gemini					Twins, male and Female
Cancer					Crab, Anubis
Leo	Regulus	Saturn / Mars	**Nimrod** / **Osiris**	Summer, The Lion	Lion, Lion Slayer, (**Fire**)
Virgo					Virgin
Libra					Scales
Scorpio	Antares	Venus / Moon	**Isis**	Autumn, The Eagle	War banner of "The Eagle", a Nike, (**Water**)
Sagittarius					the Archer
Capricorn					Goat-fish, Osiris/Bacchus/Pan
Aquarius	Fomalhaut	Jupiter / Mercury	**Horus**	Winter, The Man	Water-Bearer, (**Air**)
Pisces					Fishes

The Western Mysteries typically have four primary elements: Earth, Fire, Water, and Air. The Oriental Mysteries often have five, adding Metal. The four elements were assigned to the constellations as follows:

Bull (Taurus - earth), **Lion** (Leo - fire),
Eagle (Scorpio - water), and **Man** (Aquarius - air).

The **four pillars, or four corners, of the earth** are the four points of the two equinoxes, autumn and spring, and the two solstices, winter and summer. The reference to, and depiction of, the "**Four Pillars**" of the earth are very common. Circa BC 2600 these four astronomical events were in Taurus, Leo, Scorpio, and Aquarius. Said another way, the four corners of the earth are "**The Bull**", "**The Lion**", "**The Eagle**", and "**The Man**".

It is very important to note that these same four "**Living Creatures**" are described in Revelation 4:7, as surrounding the "**Throne of God**", the YHWH. Also review Ezekiel 1:10:

> "Their faces looked like this: Each of the four had the **face of a man**, and on the right side each had the **face of a lion**, and on the left the **face of an ox**; each also had the **face of an eagle**."

Similarities and parallel imagery is expected to be found between the two systems of worship. **The religious system which is false, a lie, will try to duplicate the real system as much as possible to maintain its credibility**.

Today, the four pillars of the Earth have shifted up the above table's rows by two constellations. For example, the winter solstice is now in Sagittarius.

Why is the Symbol of Scorpio Also an Eagle?

With even deep investigation it is realized that the reason for the Eagle symbol association with Scorpio has been lost, at least to the general public. It is not enough just to understand that some scorpions can fly. You can find 'YouTube' videos on these insects.

Winged Scorpion.

<u>A Proposal: as an educated "Guess"</u>:
Please be aware that there are different Zodiac symbols used in different cultures. For example, the Chinese Zodiac's symbols are very different than our Western Zodiac. Further, the Zodiacs of the Babylonian, the Egyptian, and the Jewish-tradition each use some differing symbols to depict the various constellations. As a consequence, **when reading Revelation, one must also speculate about which Zodiac is being referenced in John's visions**. It is suggested that the Egyptian Zodiac's symbols may be a good choice to consider. Even so, each of the non-Oriental Zodiacs depicts Scorpio as a Scorpion. It is often speculated that a more ancient Zodiac must have depicted the constellation Scorpio as an Eagle or flying god.

<u>There is another possibility</u>. In the Babylonian Zodiac there is a sub-constellation near Scorpio that looks like a winged god with serpents.

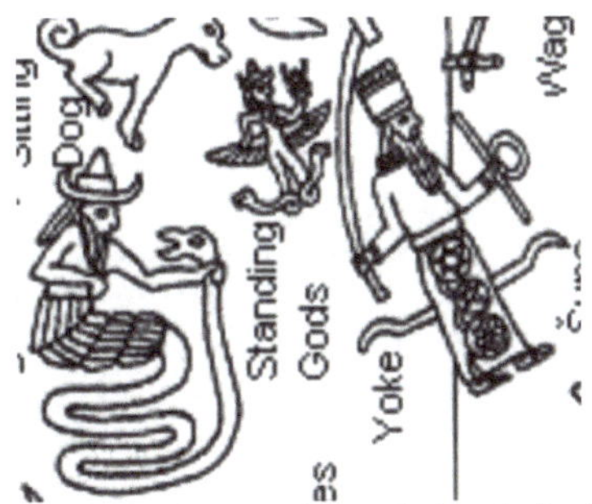

An artist's depiction of a section of the Babylonian Zodiac.
Zoomed In: a Winged "god", **a Nike.**

When the sun is in Scorpio, this sub-constellation of a winged Nike is also in celestial alignment. This symbol could be "**The Eagle**", at least in concept, which is mysteriously associated with Scorpio.

Isis is associated with Scorpio, and
is often depicted as having wings as "**The Eagle**".

APPENDIX C: More Details About The Gods

Each god in the Mysteries has many stories written about them. The names of a god change by language, and most importantly, they change based on the role or duty or what they are doing in the story. For example, in the same Roman Myth Isis can be called Cybele, as the wife of Saturn, and also be called Rhea, as the mother of Jupiter-puer (Horus, Cupid). Following are some of the more important details told about each god.

NOAH

Noah was not a god of the Mysteries, but is included as he and his son Shem are depicted as the "bad guys" in many of the Myths of the Mysteries. Often you can tell who is in a picture or statue by the primary symbols they are holding or wearing. For Noah, his primary symbols are the "**Long Fish-Tail**", a "**Dolphin-Like Fish**", and a staff.

Noah with a "**Long Fish-Tail**" and a "**Winged Staff**" (without Serpents).

Noah with a "**Long Fish-Tail**" holding a "**Dolphin-Like Fish**".

Remember the above scene is a depiction made by some artist thousands of years after the fact. However, "**The Club**" is a primary symbol for Nimrod/Heracles. The scene is showing Nimrod as forcing Noah to "go-on".

The "**Trident Staff**" is a primary symbol of Cush. Cush is shown telling his son Nimrod to drive Noah out.

Noah's Primary symbols are:

- A "**Long Fish-Tail**".
- A "**Dolphin-Like Fish**".
- A "**Centaur** ", as he and/or Shem and/or their armies are often shown as Centaurs, half horse and half man.
- Centaurs are almost always shown as "the losers" in a fight.

HAM

Since all of Ham's titles, names, property, wives, and servants became the property and attributes of Cush, it is very difficult to know when a story or picture is depicting Ham or Cush. Many Sumerian, and some of the Babylonian, depictions seem to be describing Ham. When an ancient text uses the name "**Anu**", it is probably talking about Ham, but not always, as Cush got that name too. Things to know about Ham/Anu are:

- Anu wore a royal tiara (divine headdress). This tiara is often a tiered hat, having <u>three to seven</u> tiers.
- He is the head of the "**Family of Gods**".
- His symbol is a "**Star**".
- Rarely is he portrayed as being someone that anyone would make an appeal to, in a prayer for help.
- Ham literally ate his own male children to avoid anyone taking his place. Cush was hidden from him, and later "took over".

(**http://en.wikipedia.org/wiki/Anu**), and (**http://cdn.preterhuman.net/texts/other/crystalinks/sumergods.html**).

GAIA

The goddess Gaia in the Greek Mysteries is the great mother of all, the primal "**Mother Goddess**" and the "**<u>Mother Earth</u>**". She carried the DNA of Cain on the ark. With Ham she bore Cush, the first post-Flood male having Cain's DNA. Later, Gaia became the wife of her son Cush too, and thereby many storylines and Myths seem confused. Gaia is often depicted holding the same serpent-striped staff as does Hermes (Cush). **<u>This is the same staff held by the Great Dragon</u>**.

> "In Its hand this mysterious Being [the Great Dragon] bore a **<u>winged rod, entwined with serpents</u>**", (REF_A).

The Symbol for Medicine is the "**Winged Rod, Entwined with Serpents**".
The Serpent entwined **Asher-phallus**, having wings as testicles,
is joined with the female "**Egg**" (Yoni) shown at the top.
Thus, medicine for both male and female, enlightened by "**The Serpent**".

CUSH: as the Primary God

Since all of Ham's titles, names, property, wives, and servants became the property and attributes of Cush, stories, pictures, and statues are depicting Cush as the top ranked god. Cush is "**Ra**" as himself. Cush is also the "**Son of Ra** (Ham)" too, depending on what he is doing or depicting. He is also Thoth, Hermes, Zeus, and several other names, mostly depending upon what Cush is doing or representing at the time.

Also Cush split himself into both Male and Female gods, and deified his own penis and testicles. Cush also split himself into "an Earthly Man" and "a Spiritual Man". Each of these mystical entities Cush gave different "god-names". Each role Cush did or invented also had its own "god-name" too.

Cush is the central person of the Mysteries. Many of the names of the gods actually are just Cush doing or representing something differently. To explain this, understand that Cush was very much into the "intellectual-side" and the "spiritual-side" of everything. Cush intellectually separated himself into two different personalities, one for the "Earthly" things he had to do, and another for the "Spiritual" things he would rather be doing. Thus, Cush "invented himself" as two different kinds of gods, "Shu" and "Tefnut". The "**Earthly**" side became different gods of the "Earth", and did things like had kids. The "**Spiritual**" side became gods of "Light", and did things like imparting "**Spiritual Enlightenment**", being the High Priest, casting spells, and judging the dead in the afterlife with Osiris.

> 'Atum' ['Cush' as 'his own Ka'] created himself. He spat 'Shu' ['Cush' as 'his male soul'] (air) and 'Tefnut' ['Cush' as 'his female soul'] (moisture) from his mouth. Atum`s two offspring became separated from him and lost in the dark nothingness, so Atum sent 'his Eye' to

look for them [a precursor to the "**Eye of Ra**", an epithet given to many deities at different times]. When they were found, he named Shu as "life" and Tefnut as "order" and entwined them together [sex]. Atum became tired and wanted a place to rest, so he kissed his daughter Tefnut, and created the first mound ['Iunu'] to rise from the waters of 'Nun'. Shu and Tefnut gave birth to 'the earth' ('Geb') ['Seb'] and the sky ('Nut') ['Rhea'] who in turn give birth to 'Osiris', 'Isis', 'Set', 'Nephthys' and 'Horus the elder'. (**http://www.ancientegyptonline.co.uk/Atum.html**) and (**http://www.ancientegyptonline.co.uk/thegods.html**).

Cush, as Thoth, is said to have written between twenty and forty thousand scrolls, on about every subject imaginable. Thus, Thoth is the "**god of Wisdom**". Since Thoth got his great wisdom from **talking directly to the Great Dragon**, "**The Serpent**" or "**Dragon**" is the primary symbol for "**Wisdom**" and "**Spiritual Enlightenment**".

The primary symbols for Cush are:

- The "**Trident Staff**", which he replicated from the real staff which Noah/Shem had. We are told by historians that the "**Short Trident**" he holds are just lightening bolts, but this imagery is only their own modern storyline.
- "**The Serpent**" or "**Dragon**", as he had direct contact with the Great Dragon, and brought mankind all his divine enlightenment.
- The "**All Seeing Eye**" or "**Eye of Providence**", as Cush sent out (mystically) his own eye to "see things".
- The planet Mercury, and its primary symbol, ☿ , is commonly seen on serpent entwined staffs. "**The Caduceus**" Staff is the symbol for Mercury plus some wings.

Some important details about Cush are that he:

- Is "Bel", which means "**the Confounder**", as in mixing things up.
- Is called the "**Father of the gods**".
- Is called he who "**Determines Destiny**", in the afterlife judgment.
- Is called "**Kronos**", and thereby also associated with the planet Saturn. Kronos is Saturn as the "**Father of the gods**" (REF_B: Page 32). Kronos is also "**The Horned One**" (so is Osiris) (REF_B: Page 34).
- Holds the rod of the planet Mercury, as "**The Conductor of Souls**".
- "[all of the names] originally given to Cush, became hereditary in the line of his deified descendants", (REF_B: Page 121).

- In the Egyptian Mysteries Mercury is called Thoth.
  In the India Mysteries Mercury is called Buddha.
  In the Babylonians Mysteries Mercury is called Nebo or Nabu.

Cush and Gaia holding a "**Winged Rod, Entwined with Serpents**".

CUSH: as THOTH and HERMES

The god Thoth is very important in the Egyptian Mysteries. He is often depicted as an ibis-headed man writing something. Scanning any list of Egyptian hieroglyphics demonstrates how often, and with so many different names, Thoth is represented. The primary symbols for **Thoth** are:

- "**Ibis-Headed Man**".
- "**The Stylist**" (writing pen).
- Cush is the male-side of "**The Moon**".
  Isis is the female-side of "**The Moon**".

The primary symbols for **Hermes** are:

- The "**Winged hat and Winged shoes**".
- "**Hermes the Shepard**" (just as in pictures of Jesus, holding a lamb on his shoulders).
- The planet Mercury, and its symbol, ☿ .
- Hermes is almost always portrayed holding a "**<u>Caduceus</u>**" Staff.

Hermes (Mercury) holding a "**Winged Rod, Entwined with Serpents**", which is "**The Caduceus**" Staff.

Important details about Thoth and Hermes

Some important details about Thoth and Hermes are that (from REF_C):

- Hermes is the "**Son of Ham**", and is called "**The Burnt One**".
- Hermes talked directly with the Great Dragon, and thereby obtained all of his wisdom and spiritual insight. "Learn deeply of the **Mind** [the Great Dragon] and its mystery, for therein lies the secret of **immortality**". "For this reason, **earthy man** is composite [of two things]. Within him is the **Sky Man**, [who is] **immortal** and beautiful".
- Thoth is the grand teacher of all secret wisdoms, which can be known by the experience of **religious ecstasy**.
- Thoth was the author of 20,000 books, some say forty thousand.
  "Among the arts and sciences which it is affirmed Hermes revealed to mankind were medicine, chemistry, law, architecture, astrology, music, rhetoric, Magic, philosophy, geography, mathematics (especially geometry), anatomy, and oratory."
- Hermes is called: "**Hermes Trismegistus**", which is Greek for "**Hermes the thrice-greatest**", and **this is one of his most important titles**. He is the greatest of all "**Philosophers**", of all "**Priests**", and of all "**Kings**". These three titles are directly associated with the three crowns on the Pope's tiara.
- Thoth has written the "**Sacred Books**" of the Mysteries.
- Thoth wrote the "**Book of Thoth**", and revealed to all mankind the "**One Way**". The slogan "**The Way**", often heard in Christian circles, is actually **a title for Thoth's way to enlightenment**. The wise of

every nation and religion **have reached immortality by "The Way"** created by Hermes.

- Thoth is Cush as the "**Enlightener of Divine Wisdom**".
- Hermes is Cush standing on the head of "**Typhon**" (Shem), as the "**Successor of Religion**".
- "Hermes is of first importance to Masonic scholars, because he [Hermes] was the author of the Masonic initiatory rituals, which were borrowed from The Mysteries established by Hermes. Nearly all of the Masonic symbols are Hermetic in character."
- "It is however Hermes' role as psychopomp, **the escort of newly deceased souls to the afterlife**, that explains the origin of **the snakes** in the **caduceus**, since this was also the role of the Sumerian entwined **serpent god Ningizzida (god of the underworld)**, with whom Hermes has sometimes been equated", (**http://en.wikipedia.org/wiki/Serpent_(symbolism)**).

Thoth depicted as an ibis-headed man.

Hermes holding a staff topped by the "**Sign of Mercury**".
The male "**Asher-Phallus**" (with testicles) going into the female "**Yoni**", with the two heads of "**The Serpent**" on top.

Hermes Kuoon (Dog): holding staff having the "**Sign of Mercury**", as a "**<u>Caduceus</u>**" Staff, and several other symbols. Hermes is stepping on a creature symbolizing Noah's Priesthood.

CUSH: as ZEUS

The god Zeus is very important in the Greek Mysteries, and is the Jupiter in the Roman Mysteries. He is often depicted as a bearded man holding a "**Trident**", or a shortened double-Trident. His symbol is "**The Eagle**". This same symbol is very prominent in the militaries of the western world's armies. Russia uses the "**Double-Headed Eagle**" as its national symbol.

Drawn from historical records, a depiction of the "**Statue of Zeus**". Zeus has a Nike in his right hand, and an **Eagle-topped Staff** in his left. A statue of Zeus desecrated the Jewish Temple circa BC 167.

Many stores/Myths depict Zeus as transforming himself into a "**Serpent**" in order to have sex with women.

> "Zeus, after dismembering his father, and taking the kingdom, pursued his mother Rhea who refused his nuptials. But she **having assumed a serpent form**, he also assumed the same form, and having bound her with what is called the 'Noose of Hercules', was joined [sex] with her. And the symbol of this transformation is the '**Rod of Hermes**'."
> (**http://www.sacred-texts.com/gno/th1/th106.htm**).
> This is another account of the story about the rape of "**Europa**", which rides on the back of "**The Bull**" (Zeus) going to Crete (Europe).

"**The Serpent**" has been used as a simple glyph, drawn in place of writing out the name "**Zeus**".

The primary symbols for Zeus/Jupiter are:

- "**The Serpent**".
- "**The Eagle**".
- "**The Sun**".
- In Egypt as an "**X**".

ASTARTE / ISIS

Astarte is the goddess Isis in the Egyptian Mysteries. Isis has several names and titles, such as the "**Queen of Heaven**", "**The Lady**", "**Mother of God**", "**The Virgin Mother**", and "**The dove that binds with cords**". Isis has two primary symbols: "**The Moon**" and the planet "**Venus**". To be more technical, she is the baby girl:

- Born to Ham and Gaia,
- As the sister to Cush,
- Who later became the wife of Cush,
- Who was a celebrated warrior using the bow and spear,
- Who was a red hot nymphomaniac pursuing male partners at every convenience and for every advantage,
- Who with Cush was the mother of Osiris, that is Nimrod,
- Who later became the wife of Osiris,
- Who wailed for Osiris when he was executed by Shem,
- Who searched the world for the dead body parts of Osiris,

- Who was impregnated in a special séances ceremony with Thoth (Cush), claiming it was done by the sperm of Osiris' 'immortal soul body' living in heaven in the afterlife,
- Who then gave birth to Horus, the "**Only Begotten Incarnate Son of God**" ("**Incarnated Osiris**"), on the winter solstice on December 25th as calculated in the original Julian Calendar of circa BC 331,
- Who promoted the Mysteries theme of the "**Triune God**" (Osiris, Isis, and Incarnated Osiris as Horus).

Altar to Guandi at the Temple of Guandi of Jinan, Shandong.
Notice the three gods, which are "Horus, Osiris, and **Isis**".

Much confusion is caused because each of the above descriptions of Isis represents a different role, or something special about Isis to talk about. Often Isis has different names in the same story, based upon which "role" she is doing or representing. For this reason Wikipedia and many other websites have the different stories and Myths about Isis and her other goddess-names interspersed with conflicting information.

For example, Isis and Nephthys are one in the same person. But Isis is the "**Virgin Mother**" which bore Horus, and Nephthys is the "**Mother of God**" which nursed Horus. Two different roles results in the same person being presented as two different goddesses.

Isis is passing baby Horus to Nephthys (to be his mother).
On the left are Cush and Nimrod.
On the right is Thoth (Owl), Nike (Isis as Victory & Fortune), and Gaia (Mother of all gods), with Serpent Staff.
The "**Winged Rod, Entwined with Serpents**" is in Gaia's left hand.

This scene depicts Two Trinities.
On the left is Gaia, Athena (Isis) and Nephthys.
On the right is Cupid (Horus) taking the Horn of rulership, Hermes with his Mercury Staff, and Adonis (Osiris).
The "**Winged Rod, Entwined with Serpents**" is in Gaia's right hand.
The "**Winged Rod, Entwined with Serpents**" is in Osiris' right hand.

A Closer Look at the Globus Cruciger

The "**Globus Cruciger**" is an object which is associated with being held by kings at coronations. It is often seen on the top of churches. We are told that it is the symbol of authority.

"**The Cross**" going into "**The Orb**".
(**http://en.wikipedia.org/wiki/Globus_cruciger**).

The Golden Bull of 1356

Catholic Steeple

The Orb cannot be the Earth, because the Earth was declared to be flat. The "**Globus Cruciger**" is "**The Cross**" and "**The Egg**", the symbol of human reproduction.

The question is: "Who's Egg?" Upon investigation it is discovered that this symbol is not depicted by itself. That is, one hand of the monarch holds the "**Globus Cruciger**", showing the source of their authority, while the other hand holds a staff of rulership over their kingdom. The "**Globus Cruciger**" is the symbol of where the authority comes from, and that authority is from Horus, the "**Incarnate god**", birthed by Isis.

Isis is the provider of "**The Egg**". Osiris is the provider of the phallus, "**The Cross**". The result was Horus, the "**Incarnate god**", the source of the authority to rule over kingdoms.

Statue of Isis holding an Orb (Egg) Close up of a Catholic Statue

These images show Mary (as Isis) providing "**The Cross**" and "**The Egg**", to miraculously produce the baby Jesus (Horus), who has the **Trident** above his head, thus giving Jesus the "**Trident Staff**" of Horus, and the authority to rule over men. **The authority of the Papacy to rule over men is through this Mystery-portrayal of Jesus' birth**.

NIMROD / OSIRIS

The Biblical Nimrod is the Babylonian/Chaldean Bacchus, "**The Fish god**", (REF_B: Page 113). Bacchus is Osiris in the Egyptian Mysteries. Just as Isis, Osiris has many names and titles based on the storyline and role.

Nimrod/Osiris has these primary symbols:

- The "**Club or Axe**".
- The "**Horned Bull**".
- The lion or "**Leopard Skin**".
- The "**Fish-Head**".
- The planets **Saturn** and **Mars**.

To be more technical, he is the baby boy:

- Born to Cush and Astarte/Isis,
- As the son and sister of Isis,

- Who was a celebrated warrior using a club, axe, and the slayer of lions and kings,
- Who later became the husband of Isis,
- Who had the top credentials, and was thereby a High Priest of the revived Priesthood of Cain, in direct conflict with the Priesthood of Noah/Shem,
- Who physically subdued his relatives around him,
- Who was executed by Shem (Typhon),
- Who is deified as the "**Judge of Souls**" and the god of "**The Underworld**",
- Who is "**The Father**" of the "**God Incarnate Horus**",
- Who is "**The Father**" within the "**Triune God**" (Osiris, Isis, and the Incarnated Osiris as Horus),

Nimrod/Osiris is also called:

- "**Ra**", as "**The Rising Sun**". Horus is Ra as the setting sun.
- "**The Bull**" (inherited this name from Cush)
- The "**Horned One**" (REF_B: Page 34).
- The "**Father of the gods**", through Horus' descendants.
- **"He Who Determines Destiny**", as the Judge of the souls of the dead.
- The "**King of the Living**", as the Egyptians considered the blessed-dead to be "**The Living Ones**".
- The "**Savior of the World**", through Horus being his "**Incarnate Son**".
- "**Oannes**", as the killed but resurrected Bacchus, (REF_B: Page 113)
- "**Orion**", the constellation, (REF_B: Page 57),
- Bacchus, as the "**Goat-Horned Fish**" of the constellation Capricorn, (REF_B: Page 120)

For more details found in the Egyptian Mysteries see:
(**http://www.ancientegyptonline.co.uk/Atum.html**) and
(**http://www.ancientegyptonline.co.uk/thegods.html**) and
(**S: "massey_egyptianbookofthedead.pdf**").

HORUS

The primary god Horus is the "**Son of god Incarnate**". Horus is the miracle birth son of Isis, miraculously impregnated by the after death 'immortal soul body' of Osiris.

Horus has these primary symbols:

- "**The Bow**", as depicted by "**The Cupid**" cherub shooting "love arrows".
- "**The Winged Cherub**" itself, that is Cupid.
- The planet **Jupiter**.
- "**The Cross**", represented by the "**T**" shaped letter.

To be more technical, he is the baby boy:

- Who was conceived by a miraculous miracle to impregnate Isis, thus he was born from a "**Virgin Birth**",
- Who thereby was born as the "**Only Begotten Son of god**", and the "**Incarnate Son of god**", (from the 'immortal soul body' of Osiris impregnating Isis),
- Who was a celebrated hunter using his bow,
- Who was killed as a young man in a hunting accident by a wild boar, thus <u>the need to sacrifice and eat swine during religious ceremonies and festivals</u>,
- Whose descendants are gods, ruling peoples and kingdoms with the credentials of Horus,
- Who is the third Person in the "**Triune God**" worship system,
- Whose priests are enabled to offer the worshippers of Horus very good positions in the afterlife judgment.

The descendants of Horus are "<u>**gods**</u>", ruling peoples and kingdoms with the same credentials of Horus. This is why <u>Priests perform the coronation ceremony</u>, as the Priesthood has the authority to **confer the credentials**, right to rule, onto the new king. This is why everyone is supposed to obey the king, because he has the "**Divine Right**" to rule, and in many ancient cultures, he was also "**a god**" himself.

APPENDIX D: The Beast's Name and Mark

With only a minimal investigation it is verified that nearly everyone is looking for **a future fulfillment** of the Revelation 13 "**Beast with Seven Heads**". The second Revelation 13 Beast rises afterwards, and forces everyone to worship the first Beast. Many proposed answers assume that all Beasts depicted in Revelation and Daniel are the same Beasts.

Also easily verified is that nearly everyone is trying to identify someone as the future evil man, or woman, matching a name which has the "**gematria**" (assigning numerical values to letters) of "**666**". By trying to match people's names to "**666**", it is observed that there is a very long list of candidates who are proclaimed to be the upcoming "Beast", the man of perdition.

However, there is a problem in viewing the first Revelation 13 Beast as a future fulfillment. In other verses in Revelation it is expressed that those who take the mark of the Beast are "doomed", while those that do not take the mark of the Beast are "saved". Examine Revelation 14:11, 15:2, and especially 20:4. If the first Beast is a future fulfillment, then only the future believers will be "saved" and reign with the Messiah for a thousand years. All believers that lived previously are not even mentioned!

The historical evidence demonstrates that the Revelation 13 "**Beast with Seven Heads**" **has existed throughout human history**. This first Beast is not a future choice of worship, **it is always been a choice of worship**. The real problem for us is that we are so immersed into the culture and mindset presented by the Great Dragon's Seven Schools of Thought, that we cannot conceive of anything else. From childhood nearly everyone on earth is taught to believe that everyone is essentially praying to the same "God", and that our particular religion and religious practices are approved by "God" himself.

From this perspective, it is understood why the riddle of the "**666**" is hidden from discovery. It is not to the advantage of the Great Dragon to allow the answer to be easily understood. The answer to the "**666**" riddle has been obscured, on purpose.

The Printing Press Changed Things

The invention of the printing press has changed how we visualize the past. We grow up in a world which has standardized shapes, called "**fonts**". Today using "**Unicode Fonts**" there is a standardized printable character for each character in every language on earth. Using these fonts you can print the characters for the words in any language, from the Cherokee Indians to the ancient Phoenicians. We are so used to reading the ancient text as printed standardized shapes, that we forget that the original text **was handwritten using shapes we have not seen**.

For example: if you were told that the mark of the Beast was an "**X**", you would go around looking for an "**X**" shaped mark on people. But the handwritten Greek Chi character does not look like that. It does not look like an "**X**", compared to the original manuscripts and fragments.

We see the printed "**X**" shape, call it a Chi character, but it is being shown to you incorrectly, as the angles between the cross-lines are not correct. Most people can imagine the Chi character as "a cross", but the printing press' standardized shapes **prevent people from correctly visualizing what it looks like when handwritten**.

While writing this presentation we searched very carefully for a printable character, in any language, which matched the shape of the handwritten Greek character Chi. No such Unicode character exists, not in any language. We cannot print a Chi character **so that you can visualize what it really looks like when handwritten**.

As a result we created our own Chi character, but as an image, to at least get close to the shape which is seen on the original manuscripts and fragments. Thus, in this presentation this image is the Chi character: . This image is not perfect. Since they hand drew everything, there will be penmanship variations, but this shape is a lot closer than the "**X**" shape seen in our printed books. It does make a difference.

Analyzing the Name of the Beast

The name of the Revelation 13 "**Beast with Seven Heads**" is tied to the number "**666**". Most have tried to solve the "**666**" riddle by imagining what the name of the Beast might be, and assigning each character of that name its assigned "**gematria**" value, hoping it will add up to "**666**". A Gematria Table is at: (**http://www.jewfaq.org/alephbet.htm**).

But there is a question which needs to be asked: "In which language is the name of the Beast?" Not all languages have "**gematria**" values for their characters. The two more obvious choices are Greek or Hebrew, each of these languages has "**gematria**" values. But a person's name can be very different, based on which language is used. For example "John" in English is "Ian" in Irish. "**Cybele"** in Phrygian is Kubileya or Kubeleya; in Turkish it is Kibele; in Lydian it is Kuvava; and in Greek it is Κυβέλη Kybele, Κυβήβη Kybebe, Κύβελις Kybelis), (**http://en.wikipedia.org/wiki/Cybele**). These are very different spellings of the same person's name. The language picked makes a huge difference.

The Greek Gematria Has Problems

Using the Greek language to discover the spelling for the name of the Beast is logical. However, in the Greek language the same name changes spelling based on the grammar of the sentence. In Greek the names of people and gods change, as the ending characters change. For example: the English name "Jesus" is spelled in Greek differently based on the grammar of the sentence, as either "Iêsous" or as "Iêsou".

Added to this is the issue of including the article, that is, the "the" in front of a name. In English we are not used to asking this question, but it must be asked in Greek. For example, the god "Χρόνος" (Chronos), is not the god Chronos without the article, "the", in front of it. Without the article, "the", a sentence is probably only talking about Chronos-likeness things, and not the god himself. In Greek the article, "the", is also spelled differently based on grammar. Thus, "the Chronos" has several different "**gematria**" values, than does "Chronos".

Further, there are about **24 different "gematria" methods** that are used to try to add up to the value "**666**". That is, which method did Revelation 13 use to add up to the riddle of "**666**"?

Some "**gematria**" charts show the Hebrew as having values after 400. Such charts show that the Hebrew sofit "**ם**" (M) has the value of '600'. **But it is a mistake to use these charts**. The assignment of these higher values is just another method of counting, and this method was not the "**gematria**" used at the time Revelation was written.

> "Mispar Gadol [means "greater number"] counts the final forms (sofit) of the Hebrew letters as a continuation of the numerical sequence for the alphabet, with the final letters assigned values from 500 to 900". (**http://en.wikipedia.org/wiki/Gematria**).

"… could give thousands of examples of how Jewish tradition **commonly uses the standard values** for the sofit letters. I don't understand why you would challenge anyone on this point." (**http://www.biblewheel.com/forum/showthread.php?2637-Jesus-and-the-Star-of-David**).

The Stable "Gematria" is Hebrew

Because the Hebrew language does not spell words using vowels, using only consonants, the grammar of the sentence typically stays outside of the name itself. For example, the name Noah, " נח ", does not change with grammar. Hebrew letters are attached before or after the name based on grammar. For example: " לנח " means "to Noah", but the root spelling of Noah's name does not change, it is stable. Since Revelation was preserved for a future generation, it is the Hebrew "**gematria**" which can be relied upon to remain stable, whereas the Greek language may not.

The Name Written Versus the Name Spoken

Coming as a great surprise to this author, is that a large part of the obscurity for figuring out the historical meaning of the "**666**" riddle is the invention of the printing press. We are all so used to reading information that has been printed. This modern practice of reading standardized text has changed how we think about what a name really is.

Is a person named "Tom" because it is printed this way on his birth certificate? You need to answer "Yes", because in our modern world of printing presses, "Tom" would be someone else if it were spelled "Thom". But in many places "Tom" and "Thom" would sound exactly the same. The point is that we automatically associate names **based on how they are spelled**, rather than how they are sounded out. Spell a name differently and then they are someone else, automatically. But this is a modern mindset, a specific way of thinking about names. Such a mindset has only been acquired since the invention of the printing press.

Consider that prior to about 600 years ago; "Thom" may never have had his name written down at all. His name is not what may or may not be written. His name is the sound people make to call for him.

This "printing press" mindset automatically obscures what is being sought to discover the name and mark of the Beast. For example, if the name of the

Beast was "Thom", would you automatically exclude the possibility of the name of the Beast being spelled as "Tom"? The point is that **in ancient times**, before the modern mindset of having printing presses, **the name of the Beast was what you heard, not what was handwritten**.

If your friend was reading out loud to you, and he spoke out your own name, would your name be what you heard, or be what was on the parchment? The answer to this is the mindset difference. Your own name is what you hear when people call it out. If someone calls it out with a lisp, or in a southern drawl, your name would be spelled differently on the parchment, but it is still you. Thinking that your name is how it is spelled on the parchment is not the world of 2000 years ago. **Your name is what is sounded out, not what is spelled out**.

What this means is that the name of the Beast has two parts. One part is how it is spelled out, as those characters must add up to "**666**". The second part is how it is sounded out, what is heard when the name of the Beast is spoken. The riddle of the "**666**" is one part, as that is based on what is spelled out. The riddle of the name of the Beast is another part, as that is based on what is spoken out.

Solving the "666" Riddle

Since this presentation is not a mystery novel, the answer will be given right up front. The name of the "**Beast with Seven Heads**" is "**Cush**", the son of Ham as specified in Genesis 10:6.

It is manifest that the Revelation 13 account is written to a Greek language audience, being addressed to those believers living in the cities of the seven churches in Asia Minor. When the Greek language believers read Genesis 10:6, they would have read it out of the Greek Septuagint version, called the LLX. This Greek version of the Hebrew Text was circulating since circa BC 200, about 300 years before Revelation was written.

In the Septuagint the name of Cush is "**Χους**". In the Hebrew the name of Cush is "**כוש**". Solving the riddle of the "**666**" is accomplished by understanding that in the ancient mindset they would hear and speak the name of the Beast, from the Septuagint Greek Text, and then transliterate that sound into the more stable "**gematria**" in Hebrew.

Thus, the quick solution is this: The name of the Beast is what is spoken, the sound made. This sound is then transliterated into Hebrew, the more stable "**gematria**", and the language most associated with the worship of the YHWH. Those transliterated characters are then added up, and that sum comes out to be "**666**".

That is, **say the name of the Beast out loud. Transliterate that sound into Hebrew, and add up the values**.

Explaining the solution in more detail follows.
The Revelation 13 Text specifically addresses the reader who has some "wisdom". This is a riddle, so there will probably be a "**little twist**".

These are the Hebrew words of Genesis 10:6, but transposed so as to read left-to-right, as English wants words to be:

ובני	חם	כוש	ומצרים ופוט וכנען
Sons of	Ham	**Cush**	as seen in the KJV, Cush is Strong's "**H3568**"
	MH	SWK	the Hebrew letters transliterated into English
	HM	KWS	the transliterated letters as the English reader wants to see them
		כּוּשׁ	the Hebrew letters with modern "phonetic markers"
		K-ou-Sh	the Hebrew letters as English sounds, Kûsh or Koosh or Chush
υἱοὶ δὲ	Χαμ	**Χους**	καὶ Μεσραιμ Φουδ καὶ Χαναν
Sons of	Ham	**Cush**	

Above are the Septuagint Greek words, read left-to-right as in English.

The Septuagint Greek uses the Greek letter "**X**" (Chi) to transliterate the Hebrew '**כ**' (Kaf).
The Septuagint uses the Greek diphthong '**ou**' to transliterate the 'ו' (Waw).

The Greek '**X**' (Chi) is pronounced as in 'the **Scottish** lo**ch**'.
The Greek '**ou**' diphthong is pronounced as in 's**ou**p'.
The Greek '**S**' (Sigma) is pronounced as in '**s**it'.
The Greek reader speaking out loud the Greek name '**Χους**'
says '**Ch**' – '**ou**' – '**S**', and in English it is spelled "**Chous**".
Remember to make that "Ch" sound like 'the Scottish lo**ch**'.

The sounds described above may be verified here:
(**http://www.biblicalgreek.org/links/pronunciation.php**) and

(**http://en.wikibooks.org/wiki/Koine_Greek/1._Alphabet,_Pronunciation,_and_Punctuation**) and (**http://readthegreekbible.tripod.com/id8.html**).

Taking the name of the Beast as how it sounds out, and transliterating the sounds into the more stable Hebrew "**gematria**":

The 'lo**CH**' sound would have to remain the Greek "**X**" (Chi) character, as there is no equivalent Hebrew character for that sound. Nor is there a Hebrew character for the value of "**600**". But we know the answer has a "**600**". Thus, keeping the Greek "**X**" (Chi) is the "**little twist**".
The '**ou**' sound carries directly back to the Hebrew '**ו**' (Waw).
The '**S**' sound would transliterate to the Hebrew '**ס**' (Samekh).
Note that the (Shin) '**ש**' option does not work, as it sounds out as '**sh**' or '**tsh**' or a '**soft sh**' or a '**soft dsh**'.
Whereas, the (Samekh) '**ס**' sounds out as the '**S**', as in '<u>s</u>it'.
(**http://www.edgesensor.com/feast/ancient.html**, "Phonetics of Ancient Hebrew").

Thus, the "**gematria**" characters to add up are:

'Ch'	'ou'	'S'		
'X'	'ו'	'ס'		('Chi', 'Waw', 'Samekh')
600	6	60	= **666**	

The Greek name of the "**Beast with Seven Heads**" is: "<u>**Chous**</u>", the "**Cush**" of Genesis 10:6.

The "616" Fragment

A Coptic fragment has been found which writes Revelation 13:18 as "**616**". Many have taken the opportunity to provide their thoughts on this singular and incomplete fragment. For an excellent analysis of this fragment go to: (**hermeneutics.stackexchange.com/questions/11603/what-is-the-original-number-of-the-beast**, Evaluation of Divergent Text in David Robert Palmer's "New English Translation from the Greek").

Assuming that this fragment is not a mistake, and assuming that the copyist knew what he was doing, it appears that the copyist added his own words to the original text, to help people out. After copying the words "six hundred and sixty six" (missing from the fragment), he added that this was to be interpreted as "**Or X I C**", ("or 616").

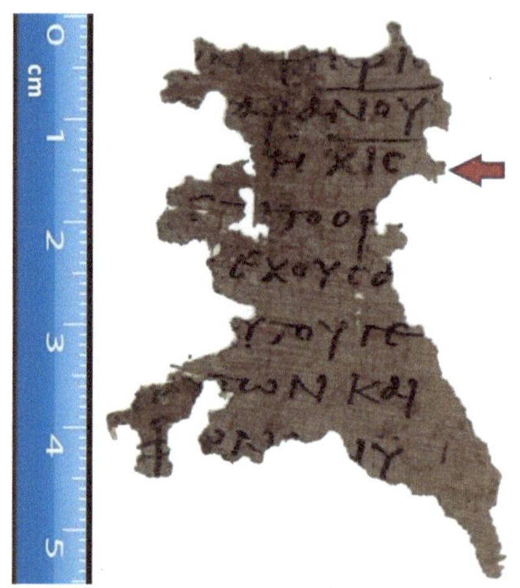

Coptic "**Papyrus P115**", written circa AD 250.
Shows "H X I C" that is "Or-else 6 1 6".
(**http://en.wikipedia.org/wiki/Number_of_the_beast**).
Note that the '**I**' looks like it may have been a '**٦**'.

The Greek letter '**C**' is called a "**Digamma**", and has the sound of our English '**S**'. The Digamma was part of the original archaic Greek alphabet, and how it was drawn went through significant changes over time, (**http://en.wikipedia.org/wiki/Digamma**).

In fact, most Greek fragments and manuscripts demonstrate that the letter '**C**' was consistently used for the letter '**Σ**' (Sigma) which is also pronounced as an '**S**'. Here are two fragment examples:

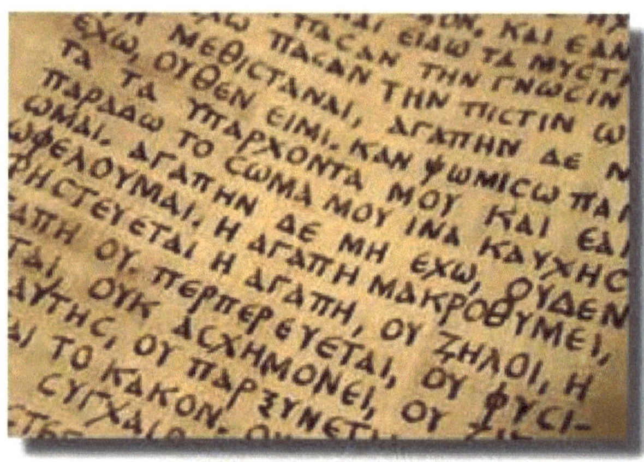

Greek Manuscript of 1st Corinthians 13

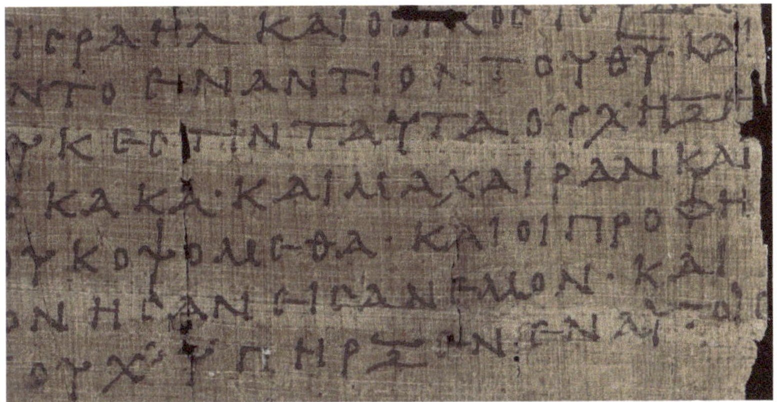

Both were written in the 2nd or 3rd century AD.

To view hundreds of Greek fragments, from the 2nd Century onwards, go to this website: (**http://ww.csntm.org/manuscript/zoomify/Rahlfs_966?image=Rahlfs_966_001a_k.jpg&page=0#viewer**), or (S: “**Rahlfs_966**”).

Thus, if the copyist was counting in Greek, then the value becomes:

‘X’ **‘I’** **‘C’**
600 10 6 (‘**C**’ is a Digamma having a value of ‘6’)
and in Greek spoken out loud as “**Kis**”.

However, if the copyist <u>was counting in Hebrew</u>, then the value becomes:

‘X’ **‘I’** **‘C’**
‘X’ ‘Waw’ ‘S’
‘X’ ‘ו’ ‘ס’ (‘Chi’, ‘Waw’, ‘Samekh’)
600 6 60 = **666**
and in Greek spoken out loud as “**Chous**”.

Thus, this fragment could be a “second-witness” that the name of the Beast is the man “**Chous**” (Cush).

The Marks within The Beast's Name

Most understand that a "mark" is an image etched or stamped onto something. According to Revelation 13, the "**Mark of the Beast**" is essentially an image etched, or painted, or stamped onto a person's forehead or hand. The Greek name of the Beast, "**Chous**", **provides the images that have been used throughout history to mark people and objects in religious ceremonies**. The Beast has Seven Heads, so there should be seven marks that the Great Dragon has used to mark his shrines and worshippers.

Remembering that Revelation was written before the printing press, so that the images of the Greek characters are what were handwritten, look at the characters of the Beast's name as figures, as hand drawn shapes, as religious imagery that could be painted onto people. What do you see when you look at these characters, looking at them as "marks" that people have used in religious ceremonies?

Χ	ο	υ	ς	"**Chous**" (Cush) as seen via printing
Χ	**Ο**	**Υ**	**Σ**	the name as seen as printed shapes
✗	**Ο**	**Υ**	**C**	the name as closer to handwritten marks

Nearly all of the Greek fragments (two examples are shown above) demonstrate that:

The (Chi) ' **Χ** ' was drawn as a right-angled ' **†** ', tilted at a 45° angle.

That is, "**The Cross**" at a 45° angle, **✗** .

The (Omicron) ' **Ο** ' was drawn as an oval, not a circle.

The ' **Ο** ' was originally drawn as an "**Eye**"

(**http://en.wikipedia.org/wiki/Proto-Sinaitic_script**) and

(**http://en.wikipedia.org/wiki/Phoenician_alphabet**)

The (Upsilon) ' **Υ** ' or ' **υ** ' was drawn as ' wings on a pole '.

The (Sigma) ' **Σ** ' or ' **ς** ' was drawn as the ' **C** '.

The (Xi) ' **Ξ** ' or ' **ξ** ' was drawn more like an 'eye', two eye-lids with a pupil in the middle.

Visualize these marks the Greek readers would see, when they looked at the name of the Beast. What they saw as **the marks making up the Beast's name are these**:

✗ Ο Υ C

These four marks also match the "**Four Pillars of the Earth**" circa BC 2600:

"**The Bull**" "**The Lion**" "**The Eagle**" "**The Man**"
(Zeus as a Serpent)

These same markings are the subparts depicted on “**The Caduceus**”, which is one of the primary symbols of Cush. Other names of “**The Caduceus**” are the “**Rod of Mercury**” and the “**Staff of Hermes**”. Both Mercury and Hermes are other names for Cush. That is, the “**Symbol of Cush**” is “**The Caduceus**”, and that symbol is made up of four subparts, and **those subparts are these very same handwritten markings** of the Greek name for Cush.

Relief depicting Hermes holding “**The Caduceus**”.

Roman Coin BC 69.

The subparts, or Marks, on the above “**Caduceus**” are:

✗ ϒ O C

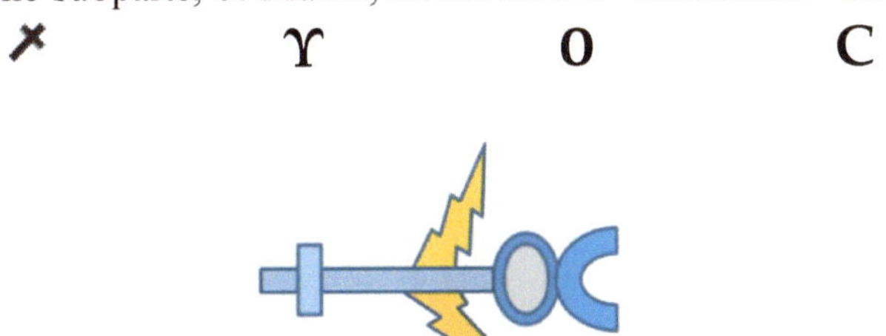

This art shows the typical Markings of “**The Caduceus**”

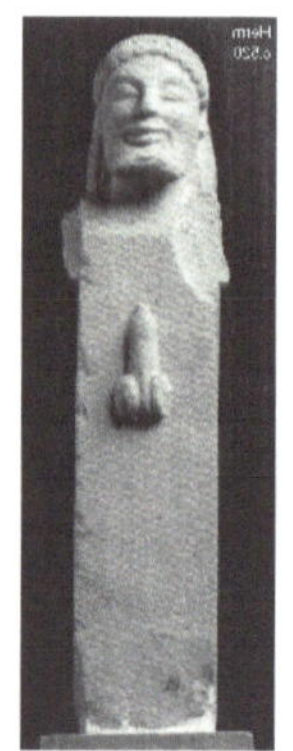

BC 69 Coin “**Caduceus**” Enlarged A Greek “**Herma**”

With some apology, the above “**Herma**” is shown. It is vital to understand visually, how the orbs at the bottom of the “**Caduceus**” shaft, form the phallus symbol. Size does not matter, it is still the “✗”.

The “ **C** ” subpart is the “**Two Serpent Heads**”:

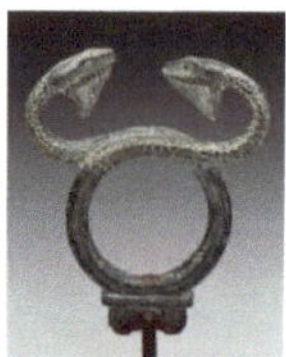

The C-shape on a Caduceus

The C-shaped Jade-Totem
<u>of Chinese Hongshan</u>

Hermes with a “**Caduceus**” having a different arrangement of Marks.

✗ **O** **C** **ϒ**

The subparts forming "**The Caduceus**" are the same four Greek characters in the name of "**Chous**" (Cush). Each subpart has its own symbolic meaning. It appears that there is no fixed order in which the subparts can be arranged. Thus, it is discovered that the ancient depictions of "**The Caduceus**" found in the different Mysteries and Myths have differing configurations of the four Marks of the name of the Beast, "**Chous**".

A Closer Look at the Caduceus

The Caduceus is Latin, and is called a "**Kerykeion**" in Greek. This rod was used by the priests of the ancient "**Eleusinian Mysteries**", circa BC 1600. The meaning of "**The Caduceus**" is a person's dedication to the "ascension of soul" into the "world of Light and Truth". "**The Caduceus**" represents the spiritual power to ascend beyond the mundane into the higher consciousness. The wings are "**Eagle's Wings**", and signify the "flight of the soul" into the "celestial sphere". Each differing arrangement of the symbols on the staff depicts different mystic symbolisms of the various connections to both energies and hidden anatomy parts,
(**http://www.avatarpoint.com/caduceus.html**).

For a history of "**The Caduceus**" depictions, in many cultures go to:
(**http://www.sacred-texts.com/sym/mosy/index.htm**).

From ancient times "**The Caduceus**" is depicted using **the exact same four Marks that are in the name of the Beast**, just in different arrangements.

The typical "**Caduceus**" will have a "**Winged Rod, Entwined with Serpents**", plus "**The Cross**" " **†** ", plus a "**Yoni**" or "**Egg**" or both. Each part represents different symbolism, so "**The Caduceus**" changes appearance based on which symbolism is being depicted. Thus, the order of the symbols shown on a "**Caduceus**" does not change the fact that it is a "**Caduceus**". The simple "**Caduceus**" will have the shaft " **†** " shape going into the "**Yoni**" or "**Egg**", plus "**Two Serpent**" heads forming the appearance of the letter "**C**".

Roman Coin BC 83: simple "**<u>Caduceus</u>**", the " **†** " going up into a "**Yoni**", with Serpents.

Roman Coin AD 74: "Pontif Maxim", showing a winged "**<u>Caduceus</u>**".

Saint Thomas Cross as a "**<u>Caduceus</u>**"
"**The Cross**" going down into a small "**Egg**", with two Serpents looking up. Notice the winged "**Nike**" above the "**The Cross**".

Other Examples of these Marks

The "**Sign of Mercury**", ☿ , is:

"**The Cross**" and "**The Yoni**" and "**The Serpent**".

The "**Herald's Rod of Hermes**": is:

"**The Wings**" as testicles, into "**The Yoni**", and "**The Serpents**".

The ancient staffs of Hermes and Mercury, whatever the Myth, **use these same four Marks** which make up the name of the Beast, "**Chous**".

A Closer Look at The Beast's Marks

It is important to understand that there are hundreds of images and symbols used by the seven "**Schools of Thought**" of the Beast. Further, each image and symbol may have several different meanings, based on which Mystery and storyline is being depicted. It is not any problem to find religious images used historically, and then call them "**Marks of the Beast**", and then assign hidden meanings, mystical concepts, and symbolism to them. Even so, this is not the case with the four Marks of "**Chous**".

Each of the four Marks in the name of "**Chous**" has direct historical evidence of being used by one or more of the Seven Heads of the Great Dragon. Not just "used", but **are historically known symbols that mark people as worshippers of that "School of Thought"**. That is, when you see a symbol being marked onto a person, you know which religion they belong to, because you recognize the symbol being used.

✗	O	ϒ	C
"The Cross"	**"The Eye"**	**"The Wings"**	**"The Serpent"**
"The Phallus"	**"The Yoni"**	**"The Eagle"**	**"Cush/Wisdom"**

From these four Marks, there are seven primary Markings that have been used by the Great Dragon to specifically mark his worshipers, ceremonies, and objects. Each Marking has its own symbolism within the different Mysteries.

1	✗	**"The Cross"**	shown in many forms, it is the phallus
2	O	**"The All Seeing Eye"**	when shown as an eye
3	O	**"The Female Yoni"**	when shown as a flattened circle
4	O	**"The Egg"**	when shown as a circle, the 'egg' of female ovulation
5	ϒ	**"The Wings"**	shown as wings, or as a Nike such as an Eagle or Angel
6	C	**"The Serpent"**	shown as two snakes, or as one snake eating its own tail
7	C	**"The Dragon"**	shown as a Serpent-like Winged Dragon

A Closer Look at the Seven Marks

Of major importance is **to emphasize a striking difference between the YHWH and the Great Dragon**. **The YHWH does not have His priests mark His worshippers during ceremonies, while the Great Dragon does**!

To be emphasized is that **there is no instruction** in the Hebrew/Aramaic Text that tells the worshippers of the YHWH **to let His human priests mark them with some symbol**, anywhere on the body. The **practice of marking worshippers** on their foreheads or hands, **whether by paint or by tattoo,** is a specific law of the Great Dragon. This practice is not done by the priests/agents of the YHWH. The YHWH does have His angles mark His servants (Ezekiel 9:4, Revelation 14:1), but such marking are done by angels, and are done for specific prophetic circumstances. **Only the Great Dragon's agents mark his worshippers during ceremonies**!

With some investigation it is verified that each of these seven Markings have been used **throughout history** by one or more of the Seven Heads of the Beast. This means that **each generation has had the choice to take the Mark of the Beast**, or not.

1 ✗ "**The Cross**": is the image used to symbolize the male phallus of a god. Other images are also used, such as the Trident and Fleur-de-Lis.

Hindu Ganesha with Trident Mark on "**The Third Eye**".

2 **O** "**The All Seeing Eye**": is the image used to symbolize the Great Dragon as the Supreme Being, knowing everything and being everywhere. Other images are also used, such as the Egyptian "**Eye of Ra**" and the Masonic "**G**".

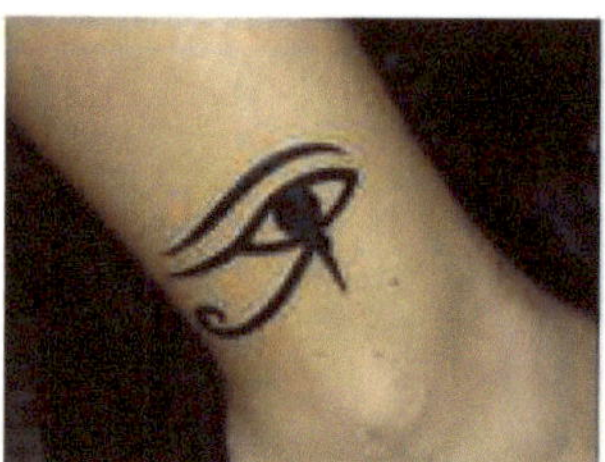

Tattoo on the hand, the Egyptian "**Eye of Ra**".

3 **O** "**The Female Yoni**": shown as a slightly flattened circle, is the image used to symbolize the female vulva, with the implication of sexual intercourse. Other images are also used, such as the Hindu "**Lingam and Yoni**".

The Hindu Shiva with the "**Lingam**" and "**Yoni**" on his forehead.

4 **O** "**The Egg**": shown as a simple circle or sphere, is the image used to symbolize the female vulva, with the implication of providing the egg to produce children. Other images are also used, such as the Masonic Square.

The Square, depicted upright like a "**V**", represents the female Vulva.

5 **ϒ** "**The Wings**": is the image used to symbolize the "flight of the soul" into the "celestial sphere" of spiritual enlightenment, with the implication of having the personal self discipline and spiritual power to succeed. Other images are the "**Eagle**", "**Nike**" or "**Cupid**".

Augustus Caesar Coin, a Nike on Orb, "Victory" or "Good Fortune".

6 **C** "**The Serpent**": is the image of two intertwining snakes, or one snake eating its own tail. These are used to symbolize the providing of superior "**Spiritual Enlightenment**", with the implication the receiving person is welcoming it.

7 **C** "**The Dragon**": is the image of a Serpent-like Winged Dragon, and is used to symbolize "Good Fortune" and "Spiritual Help". In the Chinese culture "**The Dragon**" is not quite the same as is "**The Serpent**" in western culture. Also, it is not synonymous with the Great Dragon, as might be expected. "**The Dragon**" is more of a "**magical power**" that is used to provide help, both physically and spiritually.

The "**Mark of the Beast**" that is physically placed onto people is often one of the four Greek characters within the name of "**Chous**". But the Mark can be one of the other alternative images. These alternative Marks essentially mean the same thing. Taking the Mark means that the person is marked out as belonging to one of the Seven Heads of the Beast, and worships the Great Dragon through one or more of his agents.

What this means is that you do not look for a specific Mark, like a "**666**" symbol. **People are already religiously marking themselves every day, and have been doing so throughout history**. The marking images vary by "**School of Thought**". Being marked identifies which Head you worship through. But whatever the marking symbol looks like, it means that you are a member of the Great Dragon's worship system, and following him through his agents.

For information on these same "**Marks of the Beast**" being used by the American Indian Shamans, go to: (**http://www.warpaths2peacepipes.com/native-american-symbols/shaman-symbol.htm**), and also search for "**Shaman Symbols**".

The Beast Mark of "The Cross"

The "**Sign of the Cross**" is a dominant symbol within the seven "**Schools of Thought**" of the Beast. The "**Sign of the Cross**" is the most prominent symbol of the Papal System. "**The Cross**", in all its many forms, is seen almost everywhere on earth.

Babylonian Panel and the Pope's Uniform.
The same Crosses depicted on both uniforms.

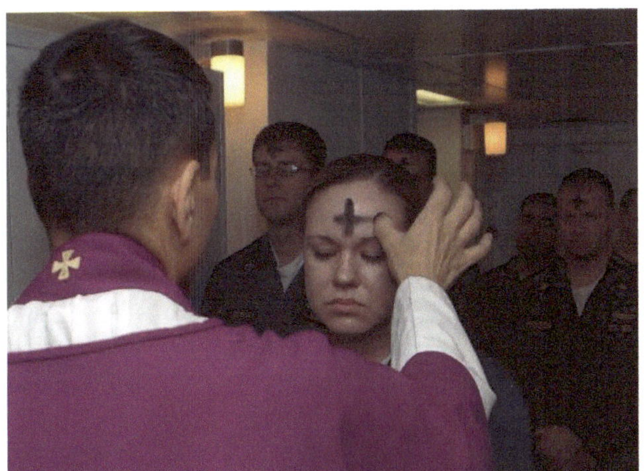

Papal Ceremony: Marking worshippers with "**The Cross**".

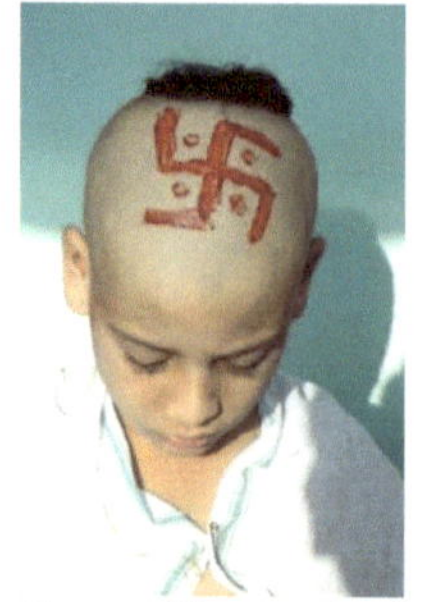

Hindu child with a Swastika Cross. Done during his Upanayana ceremony.

Because "**The Cross**" has been used by so many cultures throughout history, several other symbols are also used to represent the same concept. For examples: the "**Trident Staff**" and "**Fleur-de-Lis**" are also used as a phallic ✗ symbol:

Hindu Shrine: Sivalingam at the Sri Meenakshi Temple in Madurai.
The "**Trident Staff**" is held up as a male phallus in the right hand.
"**The Yoni**" is held up as a female vulva in the left hand.

Fleur-de-Lis on top of "**The Egg**"
The "**Fleur-de-Lis**" is held up as a male phallus.
"**The Egg**", the female vulva, is below.

The world is very familiar with worshippers being marked on their foreheads with the "**Sign of the Cross**". In the future, when it is time to take the "**Mark of the Beast**" so that you can buy and sell, people within each of the Seven Heads of the Beast are already accustomed to the idea of accepting the "**Sign of the Cross**".

The Beast Mark of "The Serpent"

The "**The Serpent**", also depicted as a "**Winged Dragon**", is a dominant symbol within the seven "**Schools of Thought**" of the Beast. With only a minimal investigation it is verified that the "**The Serpent**", in all of its forms, is seen almost "everywhere".

> "The serpent, or snake, is one of the oldest and most widespread mythological symbols. The word is derived from Latin "serpens", a crawling animal or snake. Snakes have been associated with some of the oldest rituals known to humankind, and represent dual expressions of good and evil", (**http://en.wikipedia.org/wiki/Serpent_(symbolism)**).
>
> "Each [Roman] cohort had for its own ensign the serpent or dragon, which was woven on a square piece of cloth 'textilis anguis' ", (**http://en.wikipedia.org/wiki/Aquila_(Roman)**).

Previous images provided herein have already shown examples of "**The Serpent**" being depicted on statues, coins, and icons. Here are a few more examples which may be surprising:

Archbishop of the Greek Orthodox Archdiocese of America, reads a prayer as worshippers bow down to "**The Cross**".

At a distance, what looks like "**The Cross**"
is actually "**The Serpents**" forming the "**C**" (or Sigma '**Σ**').
The real Cross is very small on top

A Staff of a Russian Christian Bishop.

Archbishop of Rio De Janeiro,
with Two Serpent-like bodies on the vest.

Circa BC 210, Xian Men Riding Dragons
(**http://en.wikipedia.org/wiki/Xian_(Taoism)**)

Oriental culture puts Dragons in tombs as a help to get to Heaven.
(S: "**full text of worship of the dead**").

The Beast Mark of "The All Seeing Eye"

The "**All Seeing Eye**" is the most dominant symbol of all Seven Heads of the Beast. The "**All Seeing Eye**" is used in each of the Mystery Systems.

At the highest level the "**All Seeing Eye**" is the mystical eye of the Great Dragon. Cush, enlighten directly by the Great Dragon's light, is its human agent. The "**All Seeing Eye**" is perhaps the most commonly seen and used symbol on earth:

> "Atum [Cush as 'his Ka'] created himself. He spat Shu [Cush as 'his male-side soul'] (air) and Tefnut [Cush as 'his female-side soul'] (moisture) from his mouth [Cush created these two gods himself also]. Atum's two offspring became separated from him, and lost in the dark nothingness. So Atum sent **his Eye** to look for them [Cush created the "**All Seeing Eye**"]. When they were found, he named Shu as 'Life' and Tefnut as 'Order', and entwined them together [in sex]."
> (**http://www.ancientegyptonline.co.uk/Atum.html**) and
> (**http://www.ancientegyptonline.co.uk/thegods.html**)

The "**All Seeing Eye**" is directly connected with the concept of the human "**Third Eye**". This mystical body part:

> "provides perception beyond ordinary sight . . . The third eye refers to the gate that leads to inner realms and spaces of higher consciousness. In New Age spirituality, the third eye often symbolizes **a state of enlightenment**,"
> (**http://en.wikipedia.org/wiki/Third_eye**).

About 1.67 billion people have a first hand daily and religious exposure to the mysticism of wearing a mark on their own head's "**Third Eye**". If the Papal System is included, as it marks worshippers with the "**Sign of the Cross**" onto their "**Third Eye**" during ceremonies, then **about 3.77 billion people regularly take a mark on their "Third Eye"**, as a religious practice. This number is not including the populous, those who only watch or know about others doing this. **There are about 3.77 billion people who actually take a mark right now**. In the future, when the "**Second Beast**" of Revelation 13 makes it impossible to buy or sell without taking a mark, then the general populous will probably fall right into line.
(**http://www.adherents.com/Religions_By_Adherents.html**).

The Hindu Shiva with the "**All Seeing Eye**" of Cush.

The "**All Seeing Eye**" on a Masonic Temple Wall.

The "**All Seeing Eye**" on a Masonic Tomb.

The Masonic "**G**" Symbol is used for the "**All Seeing Eye**".

The "**All Seeing Eye**" on the Mormon Salt Lake City Temple.

The "**All Seeing Eye**" as a Hindu "**Bindi**", placed on the "**Third Eye**".
Also search for "**Sacred Ash**" and "**Bhasma**".

"The Hindu "**Tilaka**" is a mark worn on the forehead and other parts of the body. The Tilaka may be worn on a daily basis, or for special religious occasions only. . . Apart from proclaiming one's religious affiliations, the Tilaka is also applied for the purpose of personal sanctification. To this end, it can be put on 12 parts of the body. A particular deity's name has to be recited as every mark is made."
(**http://www.ancient-symbols.com/symbols-directory/tilaka.html**).

Buddhist Statue, the “**All Seeing Eye**” as a “**Bindi**” on the “**Third Eye**”.

Buddhist Shrine, the “**All Seeing Eye**” as a “**Bindi**” on the “**Third Eye**”.

The “**All Seeing Eye**” as a Hindu Shrine.

Chinese Shaman and a little girl Marked on her "**Third Eye**"

The Muslim **"Prayer Bump"**.
Created by friction, from praying five times a day.
While easily preventable, by simply using a pillow or cloth,
it is purposefully done to be shown as a **Mark** of worship,
and has become a "badge of righteousness".

The "**All Seeing Eye**" in a Christian Church Window.

The "**All Seeing Eye**" in a Catholic Church Building in Zamosciu, Poland.

The "**All Seeing Eye**" in a Greek Orthodox Altar.

The "**All Seeing Eye**" on a Bishop's Hat.

The "**All Seeing Eye**" in a Freemason Grand Master Apron.

Masonic Coin: the "**All Seeing Eye**", as the Masonic "**G**".

The Beast's Name, Mark, and You

From the historical record, what is apparent is **how totally immersed and commonly accepted is the worship of the Great Dragon**, through his agents. The symbolism and Marks of the Beast are blatantly shown to all, right up front, and everyone is so used to seeing them that they think nothing of them.

Billions of people all over the world **routinely take the "Mark of the Beast", right now, every day**. We talk to friends, and watch shows, that automatically assert the tenets of the Beast's seven "**Schools of Thought**" as "**God's Own Truth**". Nearly everyone tells you that "**All paths lead to Heaven**" and that "**We all pray to the same God**". **But this is just not true**!

How many are out there telling you to worship only the YHWH through His resurrected and exalted Son Yahoshua the Messiah?

How many are out there telling you to keep the "Specific Laws" of the YHWH, and to reject the "Specific Laws" of the Great Dragon?

By understanding the historical evidence it becomes clear that **we should never let a priest, or anyone else, put a mark on us again**! The Great Dragon's human agents mark his worshippers, but the YHWH's human agents do not mark His! **The practice of marking worshippers during ceremonies is an obvious distinction**.

EPILOGUE

The Biblical man Cush talked directly with the Great Dragon, and started a religious system which has been infused into every culture on earth. This means that each one of us **lives in a world which, at its very foundation, does not worship the YHWH**.

The belief in the "**immortality of the soul**" is "**The Lie**". It is the foundation of the Great Dragon's religion. Everywhere people are taught that the "**spirits of the dead**" are still alive; watching, listening, and doing things. People are taught that the "**spirits of the dead**" can haunt houses, be prayed to, manifest themselves in séances, will talk to you, will tell you the future, and influence your daily astrology. We observe that "**The Lie**" is infused into almost every aspect of our culture, everything we read, and everything we are shown.

We observe **how immersed and commonly accepted is the worship of the Great Dragon**, through his agents of the Beast with seven "**Schools of Thought**". We talk to friends, and watch shows, that automatically assume that "**The Lie**" and the other "**Specific Laws**" of the Great Dragon are "**God's Own Truth**". For example: everyone knows that all good Christians worship on Sunday, and keep Christmas (Saturnalia) and Easter (Ishtar's festival). When was the last time you watched a show that said anything different?

We observe that billions of people, all over the world, routinely take the "**Mark of the Beast**", right now, every day.

We observe that those actually trying to keep the "**Specific Laws**" of the YHWH are openly ridiculed. **Such believers are presented as being stupid, brainwashed, and hypocrites**.

The primary problem is, since the worship of the Great Dragon is so much a part of our culture and mindset, **how do the worshippers of the YHWH get out of Babylon**, as directed in Revelation 18:1-5?

As a minimal effort to "**getting out of Babylon**", the worshippers of the YHWH must **at least try** to keep the "**Specific Laws**" of the YHWH, as well as **overtly reject** the "**Specific Laws**" of the Great Dragon, championed by his seven "**Schools of Thought**".

We observe that "nothing is black and white". This means that each of us should assume that we practice, right now, some confused mixture of the tenets of both the Great Dragon and the YHWH. **The world is in a state of**

complete confusion, and we should assume that we also have a subset of this confusion in our own lives.

Further, since the confusion is so pervasive, all that a person can hope to do is to "**at least try**" to worship the YHWH, in the way the YHWH says He wants us to worship Him. After all, it is manifest **that those following the Great Dragon will do everything they can to stop or diminish our efforts**.

For this reason, for us today who find ourselves completely immersed within a culture and mindset that worships the Great Dragon through his agents, we must think in terms of "**Repenting!**" **We should not think too harshly about ourselves, nor anyone else**, as the YHWH knows that each one of us was helplessly born and reared into this confused mess. But, to get out we must figure out what we need to do differently.

In order to "**Repent!**" we must know **how** to turn our lives around, and **what** needs to be changed. **This understanding comes by examining the "Specific Laws" of the YHWH**.

Looking at the "**Specific Laws**" of the YHWH as the target precepts, it can be said that we are **to at least try to live by** the precepts and foundations found in both the Hebrew and Greek Texts of the YHWH, through His Son Yahoshua the Messiah. Many of the instructions in the Texts are about community life, how to treat each other, and what to do when something is not right.

A Start to Getting Out of Babylon

From the historical research presented herein, it is manifest that we are to look towards the "**Specific Laws**" of the YHWH as the target precepts to be practiced. But there is no shortage of laws listed in the Hebrew/Aramaic and Greek Text. How then is there a "short list" of "**Specific Laws**"?

The laws listed in the "short list" are different. They have a different purpose. These laws have the specific purpose of uniquely and unambiguously identifying you as a worshipper of the YHWH, and not of the Great Dragon. The "short list" laws have a very specific intent and goal, and they can be identified.

Avoiding having to present the reader with a seminar in "Law", the simplistic way of saying this is:

> All laws have both a context and an intent, the very reason behind having the law in the first place. There are only a few "**Specific Laws**" given in the Hebrew and Greek Text, because these laws have the intent of uniquely singling out a person. Such laws demonstrate without ambiguity which supernatural being they are worshipping.

In contrast, the vast majority of the other laws itemized in the Text have a different context and intent. For example, most of these laws have the context of Israel living holy lives in the boundaries of the Promised Land and a Temple complex, and the intent of having Israel be the model country for all others to envy, (Deuteronomy 28:1-14).

Most of the laws of the YHWH are specific from the point of view that the YHWH says to do them, but they are not specific from the point of view that people in other cultures may practice the very same laws, and yet be steeped in the worship of the Great Dragon through his agents. **The "Specific Laws" have the purpose of singling you out no matter where you live**.

Further, we observe that the majority of laws also assume a cultural environment, and many physical realities that are missing in our present world. For examples, at this time there is no Temple complex, there is no buying and selling of Slaves, and there are no Levitical priests who are not getting any inheritance. Thus, we observe that the context and many of the cultural and physical realities are not the same as they were 3600 years ago. This means that at this time we cannot administer every single law and ordinance as written, verbatim. This forces us to administer these things differently.

That is, **the commands and precepts taught in the Hebrew and Greek Text have not gone away; rather they are administrated differently today, because some things are missing**.

Having the above understandings in mind, **as a starting point**, we can better perceive what we must do in order to turn around, and change our lifestyle to better match the "**Specific Laws**" of the YHWH,
(REF_D: "**/PpBeliefs_0101.php**").

Certainly we must openly, and with determination, completely reject the "**Specific Laws**" of the Great Dragon and his agents.

There will be differences in administration, as each circle of believers will naturally interpret the same Hebrew and Greek Text differently, and decide to administer things "this way", while others decide to administer things "that way". The YHWH did not make Adam and Eve as robots, so that their children (us) would always interpret ancient Text exactly the same way. Thus, differences in how the laws and precepts of the YHWH are administered should be expected, and the diversity even welcomed.

Even in the midst of all of this confusion, we have absolute confidence that the YHWH and His exalted Son Yahoshua the Messiah will see our best efforts, **and will carry us the rest of the way**.

We also have absolute confidence that the YHWH has a grand plan to undo all of the damage created by the overwhelming deception of the Great Dragon. The very concept of providing "**The Messiah**", and the promise of the forgiveness of people's sins through Him, is at the foundation of the YHWH's master plan to defeat the Great Dragon, and to undo his invasion into our paradise.

We look forward to living in the Kingdom of the YHWH, wherein Yahoshua the Messiah will ensure that all of this religious confusion will be gone.

About The Author

Mr. Wayne L. Atchison was baptized into the Body of the Messiah in July 1971 at the age of 20. He has dedicated himself to the edification of the children of Yahowah (YHWH), and the Body of the resurrected Messiah Yahoshua. He specializes in writing and teaching advanced Theological Topics and Historical Research.

Author Wayne L. Atchison

In 1979 Mr. Atchison served on a 501(c)(3) Church Board as Treasurer for six years, and has helped in coordinating 22 Feast of Tabernacles celebrations for the brethren. He gave his first sermon on the Day of Atonement in 1980. He led his first public Bible Study in November 1984, which continued twice a week for two years.

Since 1987 Mr. Atchison has produced numerous doctrinal and research papers under the pen name "**Christian Technical Notes**". Several of his articles have been reprinted by other publications. Several published books have used his research material as authoritative references.

In February 1990 Mr. Atchison was ordained an Elder in the Body of the Messiah, serving a congregation in Bonny Doon, California.
In 1996 he was ordained the Pastor of a congregation in Aptos California.
In 1996 he published the book "**The Seventh Circle in Bible Prophecy**".
In 1998 he started weekly Bible Studies in Bend Oregon, which continued for four years.
In 1999 he was appointed Assistant Pastor for the Church of God 7th Day in Redmond Oregon.

In December 2000 he authored an extensive historical research paper on the ancient Calendar of the Second Temple. This work is available online.

In 2010 he published the book "**120 Jubilees**".

Today, Mr. Atchison is heavily involved in numerous Biblical projects on advanced topics.

Mr. Atchison has served on many governing boards, presided over numerous dispute-resolutions, has led as Pastor and Elder for many different Churches and Congregations, given weekly sermons, conducted countless Bible studies, published books, organized and cooked congregational meals, lectured in many seminars, and is esteemed as an expert in critical Theological Issues.

Mr. Atchison is always willing to help people understand all sides of a Biblical issue.

TAKE NOTES

www.ingramcontent.com/pod-product-compliance
Lightning Source LLC
Chambersburg PA
CBHW041228270326
41935CB00002B/3

* 9 7 8 0 9 9 6 2 9 6 3 0 4 *